Guide to

Managerial Communication

Effective Business Writing and Speaking

Prentice Hall "Guide To"
Series in Business Communication

Guide to Managerial Communication

Effective Business Writing and Speaking

Ninth Edition

Mary Munter
Tuck School of Business
Dartmouth College

Prentice Hall
Boston Columbus Indianapolis New York San Francisco Upper Saddle River Amsterdam
Cape Town Dubai London Madrid Milan Munich Paris Montreal Toronto Delhi
Mexico City Sao Paulo Sydney Hong Kong Seoul Singapore Taipei Tokyo

Library of Congress Cataloging-in-Publication Data

Munter, Mary.
Guide to managerial communication : effective business writing and speaking / Mary Munter. — 9th ed.
p. cm.
Includes bibliographical references and index.
ISBN-13: 978-0-13-214771-2
ISBN-10: 0-13-214771-8
1. Business communication. 2. Communication in management. I. Title.
HF5718.M86 2012
658.4'5--dc22

2010049115

Editorial Director: Sally Yagan
Editor in Chief: Eric Svendsen
Acquisitions Editor: James Heine
Director of Editorial Services: Ashley Santora
Editorial Project Manager: Karin Williams
Director of Marketing: Patrice Lumumba Jones
Marketing Manager: Nikki Ayana Jones
Marketing Assistant: Ian Gold
Managing Editor: Central Publishing
Project Manager: Debbie Ryan
Production Project Manager: Clara Bartunek
Creative Director: Jayne Conte
Cover Designer: Karen Salzbach
Cover Art: Getty Images, Inc.
Media Editor: Denise Vaughn
Media Project Manager: Lisa Rinaldi
Full-Service Project Management: Aparna Yellai/PreMediaGlobal
Composition: PreMediaGlobal
Printer/Binder: Edwards Brothers Annex
Cover Printer: Lehigh Phoenix Color
Text Font: 10.5/12 Times New Roman

Credits and acknowledgments borrowed from other sources and reproduced, with permission, in this textbook appear on appropriate page within the text.

Prentice Hall
is an imprint of

www.pearsonhighered.com

10 9 8 7 4 5 6 3 2 1
ISBN 13: 978-0-13-214771-2
ISBN 10: 0-13-214771-8

For Rob, once again and always

Contents

V

SPEAKING: VERBAL STRUCTURE 85

VI

SPEAKING: VISUAL AIDS 105

VII

SPEAKING: NONVERBAL SKILLS 141

APPENDICES 160

BIBLIOGRAPHY 173

INDEX 178

Introduction

Welcome to the ninth edition of *Guide to Managerial Communication*. I am pleased that readers continue to appreciate the book's conciseness, organization, professional orientation, and readable format. At the same time, I appreciate the reader input that has allowed me to improve the book further in this edition.

CHANGES TO THIS NEW EDITION

Although I have incorporated revisions throughout the book, I would like to highlight some of the most extensive changes:

- *Credibility*: Added to the section on image credibility to emphasize authenticity and sincerity (page 9)
- *Overcoming the retention dip*: Added a section listing techniques for overcoming the audience retention dip in the middle of the Audience Memory Curve (page 22)
- *Channels*: Revamped the section on channel choice to show at a glance the advantages and disadvantages of writing (hard copy, email, TM, IM, blogs, tweets, wikis, and webpages), oral-only channels (telephone, voicemail, conference calls, and podcasts), and blended channels (presentations, meetings, one-to-one conversations, and webconferences) (pages 27–28)
- *Prewriting:* Added a new section on ways to generate information before you start writing (pages 38–39)
- *Deck presentations:* Revamped the visual aids chapter to cover deck presentations—that is, presenting from hard copy instead of projected slides (page 110)
- *Slide Master:* Reworked a new section on designing a PowerPoint Slide Master (page 111–117)
- *Labeling graphs:* Added a page on how to label graphs effectively (page 123)

- *Chartjunk:* Expanded the section on avoiding gratuitous design elements (page 125)
- *Visual images:* Added a new section on the use of photographs and other visual images (page 131)
- *Citations:* Included a new section on research and documentation of sources (page 132)
- *TMOD:* Introduced a mnemonic for introducing each slide: **T**ransition, **M**essage title, **O**rient, and **D**iscuss (page 135)

HOW THIS BOOK CAN HELP YOU

If you are facing a specific managerial communication problem, turn to the relevant part of this book for guidance. For example:

- You are speaking or writing to a new group of people. How can you enhance your credibility? How can you best persuade them? (See pages 15–17.)
- Writing takes you a painfully long time. How can you write faster? (See pages 46–53.)
- PowerPoint offers an overwhelming array of options for your slides. How can you get the most out of them? (See pages 118–121.)
- The thought of giving that presentation next week is making you nervous. What can you do to relax? (See pages 154–159.)
- People are not responding to your emails. How can you make them more effective? (See pages 58–59.)
- Your boss seems to be returning just about everything you write to be rewritten. How can you organize your ideas better? How can you write more concisely? (See pages 85–86.)
- You're facilitating an important meeting or webconference next month. How should you prepare for it? (See pages 108–109.)

If you don't have a specific question, but need general guidelines, procedures, and techniques, read through this entire book. For example:

- You would like a framework for thinking strategically about all managerial communication. (See Chapter I.)
- You would like to know more about the process of writing and editing more efficiently. (See Chapter II.)

- You would like a step-by-step procedure for preparing an oral presentation or meeting. (See Chapters V–VII.)

If you are taking a professional training course, a college course, a workshop, or a seminar, use this book as a reference.

- You may very well be a good communicator already. You would like, however, to polish and refine your managerial writing and speaking skills by taking a course or seminar.

WHO CAN USE THIS BOOK

This book is written for you if you need to speak or write in a managerial, business, government, or professional context—that is, if you need to achieve results with and through other people. You probably already know these facts:

- *You spend most of your time at work communicating.* Various studies show that 50% to 90% of work time is spent in some communication task.
- *Your success is based on communication.* Other studies verify that your career advancement is correlated with your ability to communicate well.
- *Communication is increasingly important today.* Recent trends—such as increased globalization, technology, and specialization—make persuasive communication more crucial than ever.

WHY THIS BOOK WAS WRITTEN

The thousands of participants in various business and professional speaking and writing courses I have taught want a brief summary of communication techniques. Many busy professionals have found other books on communication skills too long, insultingly remedial, or full of irrelevant information.

This book is appropriate for you if you want a guide that is short, professional, and readable.

- *Short:* The book summarizes results and models culled from thousands of pages of text and research. I have omitted bulky examples, cases, footnotes, and exercises.
- *Professional:* This book includes only information that professionals will find useful. You will not find instructions for study skills, such as in-class writing and testing; or secretarial skills, such as typing letters and answering telephones.
- *Readable:* I have tried to make the book clear and practical. The format makes it easy to read and to skim. The tone is direct, matter-of-fact, and nontheoretical.

HOW THIS BOOK IS ORGANIZED

The book is divided into four main sections.

Communication strategy (Chapter I)

Effective managerial communication (both written and oral) is based on an effective strategy. Therefore, you should analyze the five strategic variables covered in this chapter before you start to write or speak: (1) communicator strategy (objectives, style, and credibility); (2) audience strategy (who they are, what they know and expect, what they feel, and what will persuade them); (3) message strategy (how to emphasize and organize); (4) channel choice strategy (when to write use written, or oral, or blended channels); and (5) culture strategy (how cultural differences affect your communication).

Writing (Chapters II, III, IV, and Appendices)

Chapter II offers techniques on the writing process—that is, how to write faster. Chapter III deals with "macro," or larger, issues in writing—including document design, signposts to show connection, and paragraphs or sections. Chapter IV covers "micro," or smaller, writing issues—including editing for brevity and choosing a style. The Appendices provide a quick reference for grammar and punctuation.

Speaking (Chapters V, VI, and VII)

The speaking section discusses three aspects of business speaking. Chapter V explains the verbal aspects—that is, what you say—in presentations, question-and-answer sessions, meetings, and other speaking situations. Chapter VI describes visual aids, including the overall design, various kinds of individual slides, and practice techniques. Chapter VII analyzes nonverbal delivery and listening skills.

Reference

The last section of the book provides a reference for grammar and punctuation. Finally, the bibliography lists my sources.

ACKNOWLEDGMENTS

I offer grateful acknowledgment to the many people who helped make this book possible. Thanks to my reviewers for this edition:

- Cindy Crawford and Lisa Pawlik, the Ross School at the University of Michigan
- Julie Lang, the Tuck School at Darmouth College
- Elizabeth Powell, the Darden School at University of Virginia
- Irv Schenkler, the Stern School at New York University
- Nancy Schullery, the Haworth School at Western Michigan
- Sydel Sokuvitz and Kerry Rourke, the Olin School at Babson College

Thanks also to my reviewers on previous editions:

- Lon Adams, the Goddard School at Weber State University
- Kara Blackburn, Neal Hartman, and JoAnne Yates, the Sloan School at the MIT
- Kristen DeTienne, the Marriott School at Brigham Young University
- Janis Forman, the Anderson School at UCLA
- Anne Hill, the Marshall School at the University of Southern California
- Daphne Jameson and Craig Snow, the Hotel School at Cornell University
- Larry Jarvik, Johns Hopkins University
- Bill Kohler, the University of Illinois, Chicago

- Martin McNamee, the Fuqua School at Duke University
- Charlotte Rosen, the Johnson School at Cornell University
- Lynn Russell, Columbia School of Business and Prodevco
- J.D. Schramm, the Graduate School of Business at Stanford University
- Walt Stevenson, Golden Gate University
- Bob Stowers, College of William and Mary

Over the past 30 years, I have been privileged to work with excellent colleagues, executives, and students. My thanks to colleagues from the Managerial Communication Association and the Association for Business Communication. Thanks also to the thousands of executives from more than 90 companies for their "real-world" experience and insights. I can scarcely believe that I have now taught literally thousands of students—at Dartmouth's Tuck School of Business, Stanford Graduate School of Business, and several international universities. To them, I offer my thanks for their challenges and ideas. Finally, I would like to acknowledge my sources listed in the bibliography.

Mary Munter
Tuck School of Business,
Dartmouth College
mary.munter@dartmouth.edu

Guide to

Managerial Communication

Effective Business Writing and Speaking

CHAPTER 1 OUTLINE

I. Communicator strategy
   1. What is your objective?
   2. What communication style do you choose?
   3. What is your credibility?

II. Audience strategy
   1. Who are they?
   2. What do they know and expect?
   3. What do they feel?
   4. What will persuade them?

III. Message strategy
   1. Harness the power of beginnings and endings.
   2. Overcome the retention dip in the middle.
   3. Organize your message.
   4. Choose your design cascade.

IV. Channel choice strategy
   1. Written channels
   2. Oral-only channels
   3. Blended channels

V. Culture strategy

CHAPTER I

Communication Strategy

Managerial communication is different from other kinds of communication. Why? Because in a business or management setting, the most brilliant message in the world will do you no good unless you achieve your desired outcome. Therefore, instead of thinking of communication as a straight line from a sender to a receiver, visualize communication as a circle, as shown below, with your success based on achieving your desired audience response.

To get that desired audience response, you need to think strategically about your communication—before you start to write or speak. Strategic communication is based on five interactive variables: (1) communicator (the writer or speaker) strategy, (2) audience strategy, (3) message strategy, (4) channel choice strategy, and (5) culture strategy. These variables may affect one another; for example, your audience analysis affects your communicator style, your channel choice may affect your message, and the culture may affect your channel choice—in other words, these variables do not occur in a lockstep order.

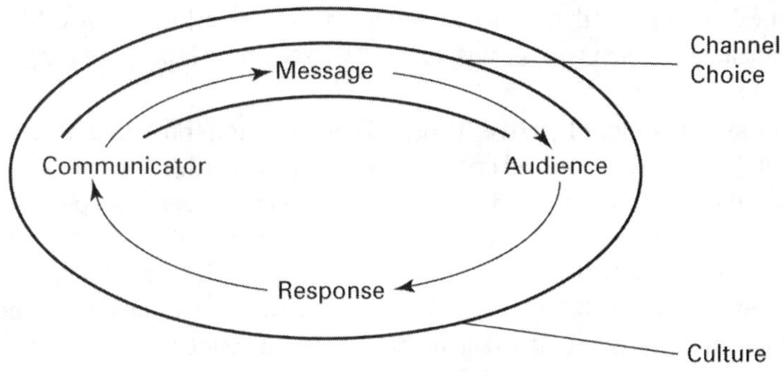

I. COMMUNICATOR STRATEGY

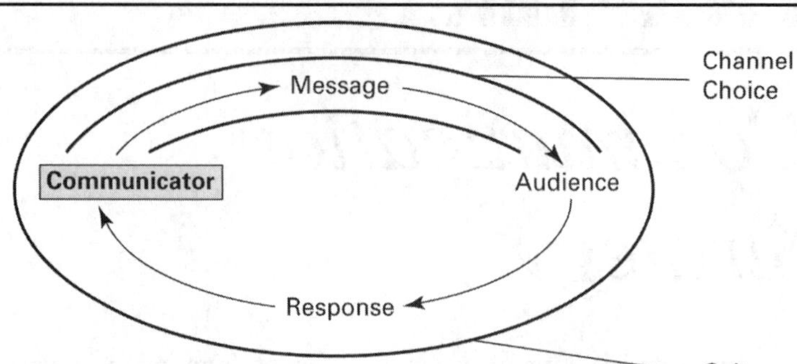

One element of your communication strategy has to do with a set of issues involving you, the communicator. Regardless of whether you are speaking or writing, your communicator strategy includes your objectives, style, and credibility.

1. What is your objective?

It's easy to communicate and receive a random response from your audience—because their response might be to ignore, misunderstand, or disagree with you. However, effective strategic communicators are those who receive their desired response or desired outcome. To clarify this outcome, hone your thoughts from the general to the specific.

General objective: This is your broad overall goal toward which each separate communication will aim.

Action objectives: Then, break down your general goal into a consciously planned series of action outcomes—specific, measurable, time-bound steps that will lead toward your general objectives. State your action objectives in this form: "To accomplish a specific result by a specific time."

Communication objective: Your communication objective is even more specific. It is focused on the result you hope to achieve from a single communication effort (or episode)—such as a report, email, or presentation. To create a communication objective, start with the phrase: "As a result of this communication, my audience will. . . ." Then complete the statement by identifying precisely what you want your audience to do, know, or think as a result of having read or heard your communication.

EXAMPLES OF OBJECTIVES		
General	**Action**	**Communication**
Update management on department performance.	Report two times each quarter.	As a result of this presentation, my boss will learn the results of two new HR programs.
Increase customer base.	Sign with 20 new clients each month.	As a result of this letter, the client will sign and return the contract.
Develop a sound financial position.	Maintain annual debt-to-equity ratio no greater than X.	As a result of this email, the accountant will give me the quarterly expense information for my report. As a result of this report, the board will approve my recommendations.
Increase the number of women hired.	Hire 15 women by March 31, 2012.	As a result of this meeting, we will come up with a strategy to accomplish our goal. As a result of this presentation, at least 10 women will sign up to interview with my firm.
Maintain market share.	Sell X amount by X date.	As a result of this memo, my boss will approve my marketing plan. As a result of this presentation, the sales representatives will understand the three new product enhancements.

2. What communication style do you choose?

As you define your communication objective, choose the appropriate style to reach that objective. The following diagram, adopted from Tannenbaum and Schmidt, displays the range of communication styles used in virtually everyone's job at various times. Instead of trying to find one "right" style, use the appropriate style at the appropriate time and avoid using the same style all of the time.

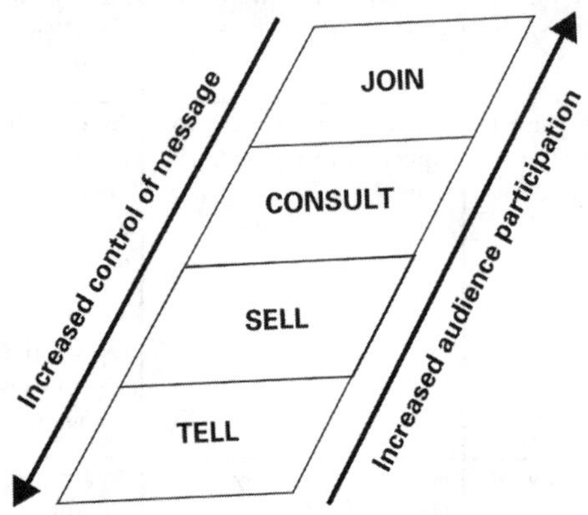

When to use the tell/sell style: Use the tell/sell style when you want your audience to learn from you. In the *tell* style, you are informing or explaining; you want your audience to understand something you already know. In the *sell* style, you are persuading or advocating; you want your audience to change their thinking or behavior. In tell/sell situations:

- You have sufficient information.
- You do not need to hear others' opinions, ideas, or input.
- You want to control the message content.

When to use the consult/join style: Use the consult/join style, sometimes called the "inquiry style," when you want to learn from the audience. The *consult* style is somewhat collaborative (like a questionnaire); the *join* style is even more collaborative (like a brainstorming session). In consult/join situations:

- You do not have sufficient information.
- You want to understand others' opinions, ideas, or input.
- You want to involve your audience and gain their buy-in.

When to use a combination of styles: In an ongoing communication project, you may need to use a combination of styles: for example, *join* to brainstorm ideas, *consult* to choose one of those ideas, *sell* to persuade your boss to adopt that idea, and *tell* to write up the idea once it becomes policy.

EXAMPLES OF OBJECTIVES AND STYLES	
Communication Objective	**Communication Style**
As a result of reading this memo, the employees will be able to compare and contrast the three benefits programs available in this company. As a result of this presentation, my boss will learn the seven major accomplishments of our department this month.	**TELL:** In these situations, you are instructing or explaining. You want your audience to learn and to understand. You do not need your audience's opinions.
As a result of reading this letter, my client will sign the enclosed contract. As a result of this presentation, the committee will approve my proposed budget.	**SELL:** In these situations, you are persuading or advocating. You want your audience to do something different. You need some audience involvement to get them to do so.
As a result of reading this email, the employees will respond by answering the questionnaire. As a result of this question-and-answer session, my staff will voice and obtain replies to their concerns about the new vacation policy.	**CONSULT:** In these situations, you are conferring. You need some give-and-take with your audience. You want to learn from them, yet control the interaction somewhat.
As a result of reading this agenda memo, the group will come to the meeting prepared to offer their thoughts on this specific issue. As a result of this brainstorming session, the group will come up with a solution to this specific problem.	**JOIN:** In these situations, you are collaborating. You and your audience are working together to come up with the content.

3. What is your credibility?

Another aspect of communicator strategy involves analyzing your audience's perception of you (their belief, confidence, and faith in you). Their perception of you has a tremendous impact on how you should communicate with them.

Five factors (based on social power theorists French, Raven, and Kotter) affect your credibility: (1) rank, (2) goodwill, (3) expertise, (4) image, and (5) common ground. Once you understand these factors, you can enhance your credibility by stressing your initial credibility and by increasing your acquired credibility.

Initial credibility: "Initial credibility" refers to your audience's perception of you before you even begin to communicate, before they ever read or hear what you have to say. Your initial credibility, then, may stem from their perception of who you are, what you represent, or how you have related to them previously.

As part of your communication strategy, you may want to stress or remind your audience of the grounds for your initial credibility. Also, in those lucky situations in which your initial credibility is high, you may use it as a "bank account." If people in your audience regard you highly, they may trust you even in unpopular or extreme decisions or recommendations. Just as drawing on a bank account reduces your bank balance, however, drawing on your initial credibility reduces your credibility balance; you must "deposit" more to your account, perhaps by goodwill gestures or by further proof of your expertise.

Acquired credibility: By contrast, "acquired credibility" refers to your audience's perception of you as a result of what you write or say. Even if your audience knows nothing about you in advance, your good ideas and your persuasive writing or speaking will help you earn credibility. The obvious way to heighten your credibility, therefore, is to do a good job of communicating.

You might also want to associate yourself with a high-credibility person, acknowledge values you share with your audience, or use another technique listed on the chart on the facing page.

FACTORS AND TECHNIQUES FOR CREDIBILITY			
Factor	**Based on . . .**	**Stress initial credibility by . . .**	**Increase acquired credibility by . . .**
Rank	Hierarchical power	Emphasizing your title or rank	Associating yourself with or citing a high-ranking person (e.g., by his or her cover letter or introduction)
Goodwill	Personal relationship or "track record"	Referring to relationship or "track record"	Building your goodwill by emphasizing audience benefits, "what's in it for them"
	Trustworthiness	Offering balanced evaluation; acknowledging any conflict of interest	
Expertise	Knowledge, competence	Sharing your expert understanding Explaining how you gained your expertise	Associating yourself with or citing authoritative sources
Image	Attractiveness, audience's desire to be like you	Emphasizing attributes audience finds attractive	Associating yourself with high-image people
	Authenticity, sincerity	Communicating openly, sincerely connecting with audience, showing appropriate emotion	
Common ground	Common values, ideas, problems, or needs	Establishing your shared values or ideas Acknowledging similarities with audience Tying the message to your common ground	

II. AUDIENCE STRATEGY

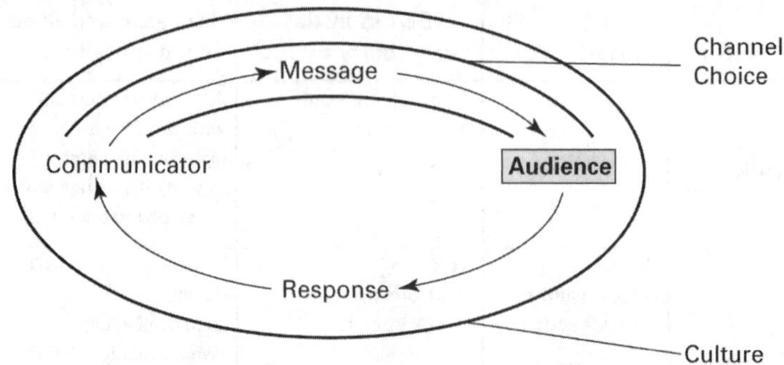

You not only need to know where *you* want the audience to be as a result of your communication, you also need to figure out where *they* are right now. Always remember Peter Drucker's wise words: "Communication takes place in the mind of the listener, not of the speaker." The more you can learn about your audience—who they are, what they know, what they feel, and how they can be persuaded—the more likely you will be to achieve your desired outcome.

1. Who are they?

"Who are they" sounds like a fairly straightforward question, but in business, this question is often a subtle and complex one. You'll need to think about who all of your possible audiences might be, even your hidden ones; who your key decision-maker is; and whom you might want to add to your audience.

Primary audience: Your primary audience is defined as those who will actually receive your message directly.

- *When your audience is unknown*, find out about their (1) *demographics*, such as age, education, organization or department, geographic location, organizational rank, and language fluency; (2) *knowledge and beliefs*, such as their background or values; (3) *preferences*, such as level of formality and preferred channel choice (e.g., email versus face-to-face).
- *When your audience is familiar*, your job will be easier, but nevertheless, take the time to analyze them. Keep in mind not only their demographics, knowledge, and channel preference, but also their likes and dislikes, typical behavior, preferred level of detail, and tendency to be challenging or withdrawn.

Key influencers: Usually one or more audience members have more control over the outcome of the communication (that is, your communication objective): (1) *decision-makers*, such as your client or customer, make the decision directly; (2) *opinion leaders* affect the decision indirectly because of their high credibility or their ability to shape opinion; and (3) *gatekeepers*, such as an assistant, have the ability to either expedite or block your message.

Secondary audiences: Do not overlook people who will receive your message indirectly—such as people who receive a copy, people who have to approve in advance, or "hidden" audiences who might otherwise influence the outcome. For example, if your boss has to approve your slides or memo in advance, she or he may be just as important as your primary audience. Or you might design your slide deck keeping in mind the people who might read it after the presentation.

2. What do they know and expect?

Before you decide what to tell them, you need to think about what your audience already knows and expects. Think about their age, education, occupation, ethnic origin, gender, and culture.

Questions to analyze might include the following: What do they know already and how much background material do they need? What do they need to know (a lot or just a little)? How much new information do they really need? What are their expectations in terms of style (e.g., formal or informal, straightforward or indirect)? How well do they speak the language? Once you have given those questions some thought, you'll want to . . .

Empathize with the novices. Put yourself in the shoes of those who don't know the terminology or have the background knowledge that they will need to understand your message.

- *Identify and define the jargon*, lingo that may be so commonplace to you that you might forget you're even using it.
- *Simplify the information.* Focus on the ideas that are essential instead of those that aren't needed to grasp the main point. Use familiar examples to explain difficult concepts. Try comparing a complex procedure to an everyday activity or incorporating several concrete examples to make an abstract idea less confusing.

Deal with mixed background needs. You may often find yourself having to communicate with a mixed audience. In these cases, you might choose to . . .

- *Provide background material* for novices, such as sending an article or CD in advance or adding a glossary of technical terms or an email attachment.
- *Acknowledge the experts* by saying something like "As those of you who have been through this before know . . ." or "Just to bring our visitors up to date . . ."
- *Aim your message* toward your key decision-maker.

Consider their format expectations. Format refers to everything from logistical considerations to communication norms. Find out what's expected in terms of . . .

- *Timing:* How long should your presentation or document be? Where does it fit on the agenda? When do breaks occur? When should the document be distributed?
- *Visual aids:* Find out what's expected and what's available.
- *Formality:* Ask how to address audience members, what dress is appropriate, and whether to use a formal or informal wording or nonverbal delivery style.

Address second language issues. Here are some techniques you can use to help the non-native speakers in your audience.

- *Check your use of idioms and metaphors.* Common expressions may seem perplexing to someone who's new to a language. So rather than reminding people to "dot their i's and cross their t's," consider asking them to "check the details." Similarly, sports metaphors can cause confusion if your listeners aren't familiar with the sport, which means they may not know that a "slam dunk" is a sure thing.
- *Avoid sarcasm and be careful with humor.* Sarcasm depends on vocal tone; it often does not make sense to someone from another culture. Similarly, humor based on puns or culturally based information may not be understood.
- *Adjust your delivery.* Enunciate clearly and speak a little slower, especially at the beginning. Use visual aids, so people can both see and hear your important points.

3. What do they feel?

Remember, your audience's emotional level is just as important as their knowledge level. Therefore, in addition to thinking about what they know, empathize with what they feel. Answering the following questions will give you a sense of the emotions your audience may be bringing to the communication.

What emotions do they feel? What feelings may arise from their current situation or their emotional attitude?

- *What is their current situation?* Is there anything about the economic situation, the timing, or their morale that you should keep in mind?
- *What emotions might they feel about your message?* Many communicators mistakenly think that all business audiences are driven by facts and rationality alone. In truth, they may also be driven by their feelings about your message: they may feel positive emotions (such as pride, excitement, and hope) or negative ones (such as anxiety, fear, or jealousy).

How interested are they in your message? Is your message a high priority or low priority for your audience? How likely are they to choose to read what you write or to listen carefully to what you say? How curious are they and how much do they care about the issue or its outcomes?

- *If their interest level is high*: In these cases, you can get right to the point without taking much time to arouse their interest. Build a good logical argument. Do not expect a change of opinion without continued effort over time; however, if you can persuade them, their change will be more permanent than changes in a low-interest audience.
- *If their interest level is low:* In these cases, think about using a consult/join style, and ask them to participate; one of the strongest ways to build support is to share control. If, however, you are using a tell/sell style, use one or more of the techniques discussed on pages 15–17 to persuade them. In addition, keep your message as short as possible; long documents are intimidating and listeners tune out anything that seems like rambling. Finally, for low-interest audiences, act quickly on attitude changes because those changes may not be permanent.

What is their probable bias: positive or negative? What is their probable attitude toward your ideas or recommendations? Are they likely to favor them, be indifferent, or be opposed? What do they have to gain or lose from your ideas? Why might they say "no"?

- *Positive or neutral:* If they are positive or neutral, reinforce their existing attitude by stating the benefits that will accrue from your message.
- *Negative:* If they are negative, try one or more of these techniques: (1) Convince them that there is a problem, then solve the problem. (2) State points with which you think they will agree first; if audience members are sold on two or three key features of your proposal, they will tend to sell themselves on the other features as well. (3) Limit your request to the smallest one possible, such as a pilot program rather than a full program right away. (4) Respond to anticipated objections; you will be more persuasive by stating and rejecting alternatives yourself, instead of allowing them to devise their own, which they will be less likely to reject.

Is your desired action easy or hard for them? From their perspective, what will your communication objective entail in terms of their immediate task? Will it be time-consuming, complicated, or difficult for them?

- *Easy or hard for them:* Whether your desired action is easy or hard, always show how it supports the audience's beliefs or benefits them.
- *Hard for them:* If it is hard, try one of these techniques: (1) Break the action down into the smallest possible request, such as a signature approving an idea that someone else is lined up to implement. (2) Make the action as easy as you can, such as distributing a questionnaire that they can fill in easily or providing them with a checklist they can follow easily.

4. What will persuade them?

Think about how you can be most persuasive by (1) emphasizing your audience benefits, (2) drawing on your own credibility, and (3) structuring the way you organize your message.

Persuade with audience benefits. Always stress "what's in it for them" (sometimes called WIIFT). To do so, (1) identify the features (facts about the item or idea you're selling); (2) apply an audience filter (analyze the feature from their point of view); and (3) create a benefit statement that explains WIIFT.

- *Tangible benefits:* Instead of just concentrating on the features you're trying to sell, show how those features will benefit the audience. Most business audiences respond well to bottom-line appeals (such as profit, results, gain outweighing cost, etc.). In addition to the bottom-line benefits, other tangible benefits may be more symbolic (such as offices, furnishings, or even just a pen or a mug).
- *Career or task benefits:* (1) Show how your message will enhance your audience's job (such as making it easier or more convenient). (2) Appeal to the task itself (such as the chance to be challenged or participate in tough problem solving). (3) Emphasize their career advancement or prestige (such as organizational recognition or reputation enhancement).
- *Ego benefits:* Enhance their sense of self-worth, accomplishment, and achievement, with formal statements, informal praises, or nonverbal nods or perhaps even hand slaps.
- *Personality benefits:* Different personalities are persuaded differently. For example, persuade thinkers with lots of data, skeptics with lots of credibility, unemotional people with rationality, and emotional people with enthusiasm and energy.
- *Group benefits:* For group-oriented audiences, emphasize (1) the benefits to the group as a whole, such as group enhancements or sense of group worth; (2) group consensus over individual preferences; and (3) group comparisons, such as benchmarking or "bandwagon" ("everyone else is doing it").
- *Consistency benefits:* People want to be seen as consistent; so if you can get them to say something publicly or in writing, they will tend to support that idea—in order to be consistent with what they've said.

Persuade with credibility. On pages 8–9, we discussed various factors that influence your credibility. Here are some techniques to apply your credibility as a persuasive tool. Remember, the less your audience is involved in the topic or issue, the more important your credibility is as a factor for persuasion.

- *Shared values credibility and "common ground":* Establishing a common ground with your audience is highly persuasive, especially when done at the beginning of your message. For example, refer to goals you share with your audience before focusing on your controversial recommendation to achieve them.
- *Goodwill credibility and "reciprocity":* A persuasive technique for applying goodwill credibility is through "reciprocity" or "bargaining." People generally feel obliged to reciprocate gifts, favors, and concessions—even uninvited or unwanted ones. So, you might gain a favor by granting a favor; you might offer a concession to gain a concession.
- *Goodwill credibility and "liking":* People tend to be more persuaded by people they like. So, taking the time to meet your audience one-to-one, to establish a relationship, to uncover real similarities, and to offer genuine praise will make you more persuasive in the long run.
- *Image credibility and emotionality:* Another way to persuade is to connect emotionally with your audience. Show your emotional commitment and adjust your emotions to your audience's emotional state.
- *Rank and expertise credibility by association:* Sometimes, rank and expertise can be persuasive. So, either refer to your own rank or expertise, or else use rank or expertise by association (for example, have the CEO introduce you or cite credible experts).
- *Rank credibility and punishment:* The most extreme application of rank credibility is using threats and punishments, such as reprimands, pay cuts, demotions, or even dismissal. Researchers have found that threats produce tension, provoke counteraggression, increase fear and dislike, work only when you're on the spot to assure compliance, and may eliminate an undesired behavior without producing the desired behavior. Therefore, threats and punishments are inappropriate for most audiences and most situations.

Persuade with message structure. Finally, in some situations, you might motivate your audience by the way you structure your message.

- *Opening and closing:* Always emphasize audience benefits (as described on page 15) in your opening and closing.
- *The problem/solution structure:* If you can convince your audience that there is a problem, then according to "balance theory" (or the "consistency principle"), they will feel "out of balance" and want to come back to equilibrium by accepting your solution.
- *One-sided versus two-sided structure*: Use a two-sided approach for a major or controversial subject, a sophisticated or negative audience, or an audience who will hear opposing arguments. This technique works because (1) they will hear your positive arguments more clearly after their concerns have been addressed, (2) they are more likely to reject alternatives explained to them than alternatives they bring up themselves, and (3) you will appear more reasonable and fair-minded. Use a one-sided argument for an uninformed or neutral audience.
- *Pro/con versus con/pro:* List the "pros" first for a noncontroversial subject or if your credibility is high; list the "cons" first for a delicate, highly charged situation or if your credibility is low.
- *The inoculation technique:* "Inoculate" your audience by presenting a mild opposing view. People are much more likely to fight in favor of objecttions they raise by themselves than objections stated and refuted by someone else.
- *Ascending versus descending order:* Use an ascending order (strongest arguments first) with an informed or interested audience; use a descending order for a less-informed or less-engaged audience.
- *The "ask for less" (or "foot in door") technique:* If you break down your communication objective into the smallest possible request, one that you are likely to get (such as a pilot program), then later you will be more likely to get the larger request. Similarly, make it easy for the audience to respond: for example, provide a questionnaire they can fill in easily, a checklist they can follow, or specific next steps or specific actions.
- *The "ask for more" (or "door in face") technique:* The opposite of "ask for less" is to ask for an extreme request that you fully expect to be rejected, followed by a more moderate request that is more likely to be honored.

You can also persuade by using the general message strategies covered in the next section.

III. MESSAGE STRATEGY

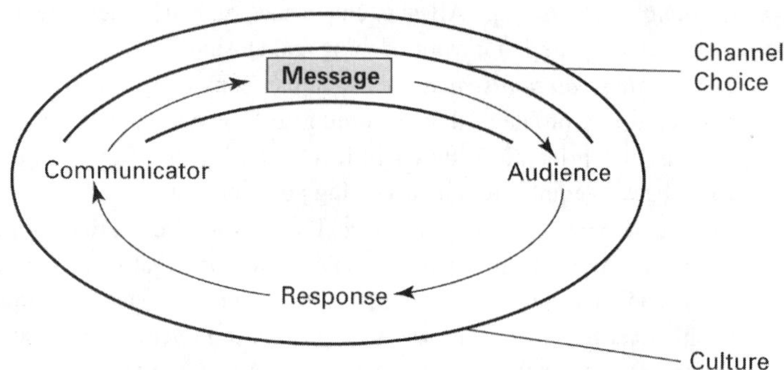

Structuring your message is a third variable in your communication strategy. Ineffective communicators simply state their ideas in the order they happen to occur to them, called a "data dump." A data dump is easy for you, but hard for your audience. Instead, stand back and think about what you want them to take away, by emphasizing and organizing your ideas. The following illustration graphically demonstrates this difference:

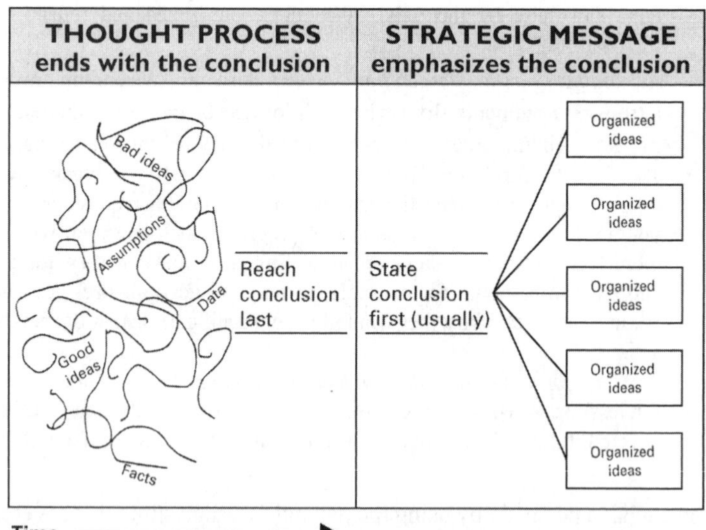

Instead of structuring your message as ideas happen to occur to you, ask the following questions: (1) How can you emphasize? (2) How can you organize?

1. Harness the power of beginnings and endings.

The following Audience Memory Curve is a graphic representation of a well-known principle (sometimes known as the "primacy/recency effect"): people remember what's first and last, not what's in the middle.

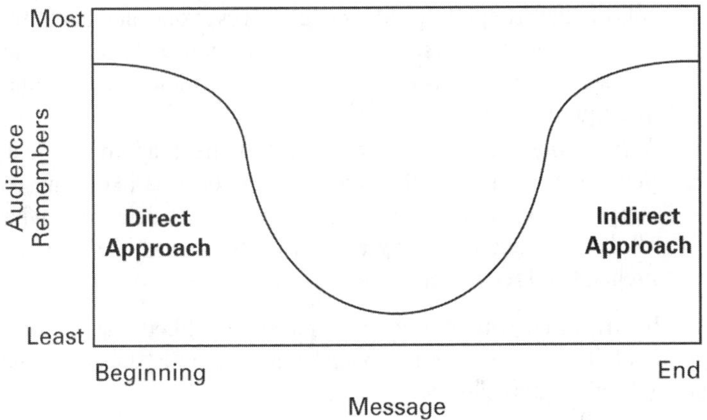

As the Audience Memory Curve implies, you should . . .

- *Never "bury" important conclusions* in the middle of your message.
- *Keep your audience's attention* in the middle of your message by using the persuasion techniques described on pages 15–17 and the retention dip techniques on page 22.
- *State your main conclusion emphatically*—at the beginning and at the end.

State your conclusion prominently. To harness the power of beginnings and endings, state your overall main point (also known as your governing idea or thesis) in the opening or closing of your message. Stating your main point up front is called the "direct approach"; saving it for the end is called the "indirect approach." In general, use the direct approach whenever possible; reserve the indirect approach only if your audience or message demands it.

- *Direct approach:* Use the direct approach whenever possible because it (1) improves audience comprehension and retention, because knowing the conclusion first makes it much easier to follow the supporting ideas, (2) saves your audience time because they understand you better, and (3) is audience-centered because it focuses on what they want to know, not how you figured it out.
- *Indirect approach:* By contrast, the indirect approach delays your main point until the end. This approach is like a mystery story; it takes a long time for the audience to determine where all the evidence is leading and they will be less likely to comprehend and retain your ideas.

Use the direct approach whenever possible. Although it may seem counterintuitive to share your conclusions first, most business audiences prefer this approach because it . . .

- *Improves their comprehension and saves them time:* People assimilate content more readily when they know the conclusions first. Surprise endings are fine for mystery readers, but not for busy executives who may resent every minute they spend trying to figure out what you're trying to say.
- *Focuses on the "bottom line," not how you got to it:* The direct approach emphasizes the results of your analysis. By contrast, an indirect one reviews the steps of your analysis. Although some audience members may want to hear about your methodology (how you researched and discovered your ideas), most will care far more about your final results than about how you discovered them; with a direct approach, you focus on their interests rather than your methodology.

Therefore, the direct approach is appropriate over 90% of the time in the U.S. business culture for . . .

- *All nonsensitive messages*
- *Sensitive messages if* (1) the audience has a positive or neutral bias, (2) they are results-oriented, or (3) your credibility is high.

Use an indirect approach with caution. Many of us use the indirect approach by habit or academic training, or because we want our audience to appreciate all of our effort and we don't want to "give away" the answer.

However, since the indirect approach is harder to follow and takes longer to understand, use it with care, reserving it for situations in which you want to soften the audience's resistance to an unpopular idea or to increase their likelihood of seeing you as fair-minded. Therefore, use this approach only when certain constraints require you to do so because of . . .

- *Audience and message constraints*, when you have: (1) a highly sensitive message, low credibility, and a negatively biased or a hostile audience, or (2) an analysis-oriented decision-maker who insists upon it.
- *Cultural norms*, when you are in another culture in which the direct approach would be viewed as inappropriate or pushy.

2. Overcome the retention dip in the middle.

Use the following techniques to alleviate the retention dip in the middle of the Audience Memory Curve.

Chunking improves memory. Since psychology experiments show that people can't easily remember more than five to seven items, you should always package your information into five to seven major chunks, then subdivide your main chunks into five to seven chunks, and so forth. Chunking your content allows you to create mini-memory curves, elevating overall audience attention.

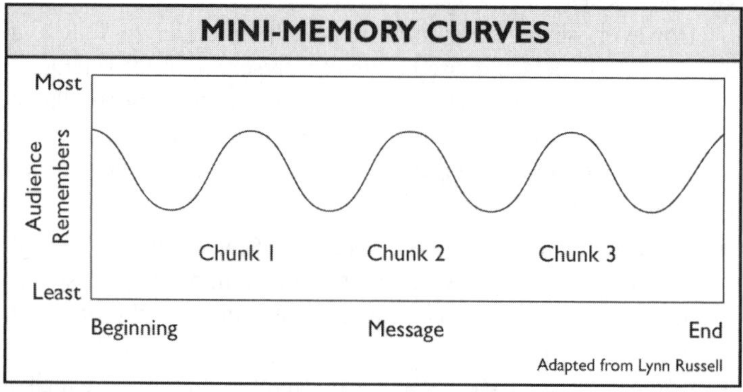

Repetition gets noticed. People remember what they've been exposed to several times. So, in a presentation, repeat the main points in your preview, visuals, and transitions; in writing, repeat your main points in the introduction and in the headings.

Flagging signals importance. The technique of "flagging" means drawing audience attention to important points by using a verbal flag, such as "if you only remember one thing, remember . . ." or "here's the critical point . . ."

The unexpected grabs attention. People tend to remember something that is unusual or unexpected. For example, in a presentation, you might dramatically change your delivery style, show a powerful video clip, or alter the pace of your presentation; in writing, you might tell a startling story or dramatically alter your format.

Visuals provide reinforcement. If people can see a message in addition to hearing or reading it, they are more likely to retain it. That's why your visual aids are so important in a presentation and why an unusual slide will stand out and why you might insert graphs and charts into your writing.

3. Organize your message.

In addition to emphasizing your conclusion, you need to organize your main ideas in the body of your message.

Common ways to order an informative message: For "tell" communication, decide how to chunk the information you've collected so that you can highlight your major points. Here are some examples of possible organizational patterns.

- *Key points:* With this pattern, you select a limited number of points and order them in a sequence that enables you to connect each point to the one that follows. For example, if you wanted to make three key points about your new dividend policy, then your ordering system might look like this: (1) investor attitude moved toward a yield preference, (2) surplus capital rendered the previous payout ratio impractical, and (3) tax changes made the new policy more desirable.
- *Key questions:* This pattern groups your content based on questions you will cover. For instance, you might highlight your business plan by using a series of questions: (1) Why is the environment right? (2) What is our competitive advantage? (3) How will we secure start-up funds? (4) Who will lead and manage this venture?
- *Steps in a process:* With this pattern, you use a chronological approach, moving through the steps in the sequence they should be undertaken. For example, to explain how to sign up for a health care provider, a speaker may recommend that new employees (1) complete all the medical forms required for employment, (2) review the new "Health Choices" brochure, and (3) meet with a benefits counselor to enroll.
- *Alternatives to compare:* Another option is to outline several alternatives and compare each one to the ones that preceded it. So, if you want to compare the desirability of different graduate degrees based on the openings in an organization, you might use this approach (1) PhDs for senior research positions, (2) MPAs for policy research and grant writing, (3) MBAs for economic research and financial posts, and (4) other degrees for nonresearch positions.

Common ways to order a persuasive communication: To be persuasive in a "sell" situation, you need to find an organizational pattern that works best for your situation. Here are some options to consider:

- *List of recommendations (direct approach):* "We can improve our growth and efficiency if we (1) change our product mix and (2) enhance the customer service department."
- *List of benefits (direct approach):* "We should use Ad Graphics as our primary printing company for three reasons: (1) they're able to meet our quality and cost requirements, (2) we'll get faster delivery, and (3) we'll be making progress on our community relations initiative by using a local printing service."
- *Problem and possible solutions (indirect approach):* "First, I'll describe the technology problems in the San Francisco and Pittsburgh offices. Then, I'll share three alternatives we can consider to deal with these challenges."

4. Choose your design cascade.

Once you have organized your material, think about what communication consultant Julie Lang has termed a "design cascade." Design cascade is the way you show your organization to your audience—combining placement, size, and font styles—to resemble a cascade flowing from left to right on your document or slide.

Example of a design cascade

FLUSH LEFT TITLE

Indented main heading

Subset heading

Example heading

Of course, a design cascade does not always have to literally flow from left to right. Here is another example in which your audience can still see how your ideas "cascade."

Example of a design cascade with the title centered

CENTERED TITLE

Soger doef retaw ellsw tnemeo stin yo teicor sretem bptse hilpen.

Main heading on its own line
Nthron osltry sirton yotad neewbet ehlt stretcat ahc hitwed hip locial koodreoy. Nthron osltry sirton yotad neewbet ehlt stretcat ahc hitwed hip locial koodreoy.

Run-in subset heading is set into the rest of the text nthron osltry sirton yotad.

Second main heading on its own line
Osltry sirton yotad neewbet ehlt stretcat ahc nthron osltry sirton yotad neewbet ehlt stretcat ahc nthron osltry sirton yotad neewbet ehlt stretcat ahc.

The chart below shows the range of design choices—from the most emphatic to the least emphatic—including placement, size, and font style.

CHOICES FOR DESIGN CASCADE More emphasis ⟷ Less emphasis				
PLACEMENT	Centered	Flush left	Indented	Run-in
SIZE	Headings 14–16 for writing 28–32 for slides	Text 11–12 for writing 18–24 for slides	Tables & labels 10 for writing 14 for slides	
FONT STYLE	**ALL CAPS**	**Boldface**	*Italics*	Regular text

IV. CHANNEL CHOICE STRATEGY

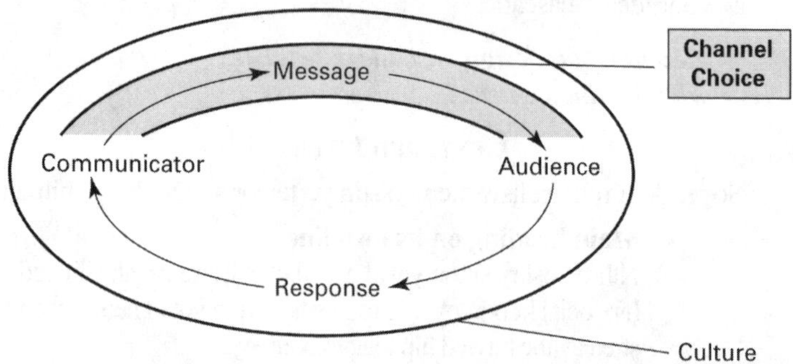

Channel choice refers to the choice of a medium through which you will transmit your message. The following four tables summarize these channels.

CHANNELS OF COMMUNICATION			
	Highly interactive, always real time	**Moderately interactive**	**Minimally interactive, never real time**
1. Written	Text message Instant message	Email Blogs & tweets Social networking Wikis	Hard copy Webpage
2. Oral only	Telephone Conference call		Voicemail Podcast
3. Blended	One-to-one Consult/join meeting Webmeeting	Tell/sell presentation Webcast (live)	Webcast (recorded) Adapted from J. D. Schramm

1. WRITTEN CHANNELS						
	Hard copy	**Email**	**Blogs & tweets**	**IM & TM**	**Wikis**	**Webpages**
Advantages	Private Detailed Shreddable	Quicker distribution than hard copy	Interactive Creates community	Highly interactive Fastest response	Collaborative writing	Potentially huge audience
Disadvantages	Rigid Delayed response	Unorganized, too uninhibited Permanent	Relies on blogger expertise	Overused, irritating	Hard to control content	No control over who reads

2. ORAL-ONLY CHANNELS				
	Telephone	**Voicemail**	**Conference call**	**Podcast**
Advantages	Private	Short items quickly	Multiple receivers at same time	"Radio show" for anyone with an MP3 player
Disadvantages	Telephone tag	Delayed or no response	Equal interaction difficult	No call-in or live feedback

3. BLENDED CHANNELS					
	Tell/sell presentation (inform or persuade)	**Consult/join meeting** (interact or brainstorm)	**Conversation** (face-to-face)	**Tell/sell webcast** (inform or persuade)	**Consult/join webmeeting** (interact or brainstorm)
Advantages	Richest channels: verbal and nonverbal communication Real time; can control audience receiving information				
	Best for relationships			Reaches different locations	
Disadvantages	Slower for audience because listening takes more time than reading Less detail than writing				

Strategic channel choice means choosing your channel consciously, thoughtfully, and carefully (in view of your objective, audience, and message)—instead of always using channels you prefer and feel comfortable with.

Consider strategic questions: Think about the following general questions before you choose a channel for your communication:

1. Does your audience have a preference?
2. How much audience participation do you want?
3. Do you want to communicate nonverbally?
4. Do you want to control the timing of your message?
5. Do you want a permanent record?
6. How much detail do you want to communicate?

Choose your channel(s): Then, take the time to choose the best channel, given your communication strategy. Or, if you don't have a choice about the channel, think about how you can overcome its shortcomings (e.g., providing hard copy along with your presentation or following up an email sent under time pressure with a face-to-face conversation to make sure it was not misunderstood or misinterpreted).

Improve your skills: For tips on the various channels . . .

- ***Writing:*** See Chapters II–IV and the Appendices
- ***Tell/sell presentations:*** See Chapters V–VII
- ***Consult/join meetings:*** See pages 95–98
- ***Webconferences:*** See pages 100–101
- ***Listening skills*** (for conversations and Q&A): See page 97

V. CULTURE STRATEGY

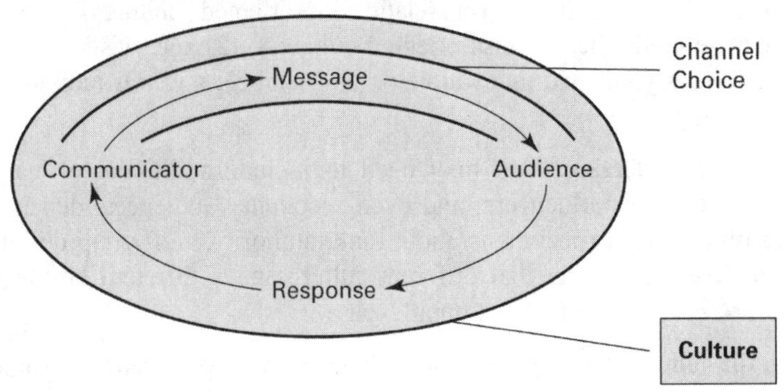

The culture in which you are communicating will influence every aspect of your communication strategy. The term "different cultures" includes different countries, regions, industries, organizations, genders, ethnic groups, or work groups. The danger in cultural analysis is stereotyping: saying all the people in a group behave a certain way all the time and using negative phrasing, such as "all British people are cold." A more useful approach is to think in terms of cultural norms: saying most people in a group behave a certain way most of the time, expressed as a behavior, not as a judgment, such as "the British tend to use formal greetings."

Time: When you are setting your communication objective, you might want to set a different objective in a culture that is relaxed and past-oriented about time than you would in a culture that is precise and future-oriented. Some cultures view sticking to the agenda and timeframe as a necessity; others are more flexible.

Fate: Think also about the cultural attitude toward fate: the objective you set in a culture believing in deterministic fate may be different from one set in a culture believing in human control over fate.

Communication style: Different communication styles will tend to work better in different cultures. Group-oriented cultures may favor consult/join styles; individualistic cultures may favor tell/sell styles. Autocratic cultures may favor tell styles; democratic cultures may favor consult styles.

Credibility: The five aspects of credibility are valued differently in different cultures. For example, think about the importance placed on (1) goodwill credibility (in relationship-oriented cultures) *versus* expertise credibility (in task-oriented cultures), (2) age, wisdom, and rank *versus* youth and innovation, or (3) social class *versus* individual meritocracy.

Audience selection: You may need to include additional primary audiences, key influencers, and even secondary audiences, depending on cultural expectations about rank, authority, and group definition. Also, remember that different cultures have different attitudes toward age, sex, and educational level.

Persuasion: Different persuasion techniques will work better in some cultures than others. Although some cultures value material wealth and acquisition, others place greater value on work relationships, challenges, or status. Some cultures value Western logic more than others. The relative importance of individual relationships and credibility varies, as does the relative importance of group relationships and identity. Finally, persuasive values and ideals vary tremendously among cultures.

Gender-based tendencies: Sometimes it's useful to think about the cultural differences between men and women. Research shows, for example, that men tend to take arguments impersonally, women personally; that men seek quick authoritative decisions, women use consensus building; that men use stronger language even when they're not sure, women use more qualified language even when they are sure; and that men use less active listening, women use more.

Message structure: In addition, cultural factors will influence your choice of message structure. Cultures valuing slow, ritualistic negotiations may favor indirect structure; cultures valuing fast, efficient negotiations may favor direct structure. Authoritarian cultures may favor direct structure downward and indirect structure upward.

Channel choice: Different cultures may have different norms for channel and form—for example, a technical department versus a marketing department or a traditional organization versus a start-up venture. These norms may range from standardized one-page memos to face-to-face hallway discussions. In addition, cultures valuing personal trust more than hard facts tend to prefer oral communication and oral agreements; cultures valuing facts and efficiency tend to prefer written communication and written agreements.

Nonverbal behavior: Consider cultural norms regarding body and voice: posture, gestures, eye contact and direction of gaze, facial expression, touching behaviors, pitch, volume, rate, and attitude toward silence. Avoid gestures that would be considered rude or insulting; resist applying your own nonverbal meanings to those of other cultures. For example, Vietnamese may look down to show respect, but that doesn't mean they are "shifty." Northeasterners may speak fast, but that doesn't mean they are "arrogant."

Space and objects: Also consider norms regarding space and objects: how much personal space people are comfortable with, how much institutional space people are given (who works where, with how much space, and with what material objects), how people dress, and how rigid dress codes are. For example, Latin Americans may prefer a closer social space; Swedes may prefer a more distant social space.

Greetings and hospitality: Finally, consider cultural norms regarding greetings and hospitality. Knowing these norms can go a long way toward increasing your rapport and credibility.

For much more information about this topic, see the *Guide to Cross-Cultural Communication*, cited on page 174.

Once you have set your communication strategy, then refer to the appropriate chapters, as described in more detail in "Guide to the *Guide*" on page 43.

- ***For writing:*** Chapters II, III, and IV, and the Appendices
- ***For speaking:*** Chapters V, VI, and VII

COMMUNICATION STRATEGY CHECKLIST

Communicator Strategy

1. What is your communication objective?
2. What communication style do you choose?
3. What is your credibility?

Audience Strategy

1. Who are they?
2. What do they know and expect?
3. What do they feel?
4. What will persuade them?

Message Strategy

1. How can you harness the power of the beginning and the ending?
2. How can you overcome the retention dip in the middle?
3. How should you organize your message?
4. What design cascade will you use?

Channel Choice Strategy

1. Written channels
2. Oral-only channels
3. Blended channels

Culture Strategy

What are the cultural attitudes toward time, fate, credibility, audience selection, persuasion, message structure, channel choice, and nonverbal behavior?

GUIDE TO THE GUIDE TO MANAGERIAL COMMUNICATION

To set your communication strategy → See Chapter I

- Communicator strategy
- Audience strategy
- Message strategy
- Channel choice strategy
- Culture strategy

If you are writing . . .

- To enhance the process of writing → See Chapter II
- To write effectively on the macro level → See Chapter III
- To write effectively on the micro level → See Chapter IV
- To write correctly → See the Appendices

If you are speaking . . .

- To structure what you say → See Chapter V
- To use effective visual aids → See Chapter VI
- To improve your nonverbal delivery skills → See Chapter VII

CHAPTER II OUTLINE

I. General composing techniques
   1. Research
   2. Organize
   3. Focus
   4. Draft
   5. Edit

II. Special composing techniques
   1. Overcoming writer's block
   2. Writing in groups
   3. Using email

CHAPTER II

Writing: Composing Efficiently

People spend a lot of time at work writing—word processing longer messages (printed in hard copy or distributed electronically), emailing shorter messages, and text messaging or instant messaging very short messages indeed. Therefore, this chapter offers you some techniques for writing under the time pressure most of us feel at work and for composing more efficiently—that is, faster.

You can think about good writing in two different ways: process and product.

- *Process:* Chapter II is about the most effective process to use when you're writing—in other words, "how to do it."
- *Product:* Chapters III and IV will cover the characteristics of an effective written product—that is, "what to do."

Specifically, this chapter will discuss (1) a general composing process to use for all writing and (2) specific composing techniques for writing under special circumstances, including email.

COMPOSING EFFICIENTLY: THE WRITING PROCESS		
Chapter section	**I. General composing techniques**	**II. Special composing techniques**
Section topics	Research, organize, focus, draft, and edit	Writer's block, group writing, and email

I. GENERAL COMPOSING TECHNIQUES

COMPOSING EFFICIENTLY: THE WRITING PROCESS		
Chapter section	**I. General composing techniques**	**II. Special composing techniques**
Section topics	Research, organize, focus, draft, and edit	Writer's block, group writing, and email

Regardless of whether you're writing a many-paged document or a one-sentence text message, start by making some decisions and setting some expectations for yourself.

- *Setting your strategy first:* Before you write, always set, review, and keep in mind your communication strategy, as explained in the previous chapter.
- *Deciding whether to write or not:* As a part of that strategy, give some thought to a basic strategic issue: should you write or not? (1) Do you have an important reason to write? (2) Do you want to solidify what may be temporary feelings on the matter? (3) Is writing too risky? Are you sure you want a permanent record? (4) Do you need to see your audience's reactions immediately? (5) Given your audience's situation, is this the right time to be writing? (6) Are you the right person to be writing this particular message?
- *Differentiating activities:* Once you decide it is appropriate to write, you will save yourself time if you can clearly differentiate among five activities in the writing process: (1) researching, (2) organizing, (3) focusing information, (4) drafting, and (5) editing. Each of these activities calls for different skills.
- *Expecting overlap:* At the same time that you differentiate these stages, do not expect them to occur in lockstep order. Instead, during any one of these stages, be prepared to loop back, to rethink, or to make changes. For example, once you've focused your ideas, you may find you need to collect more information for certain topics; or, once you've completed a draft, you may discover you need to reorganize some of your ideas. If you set your expectations for this kind of intelligent flexibility, you will take it in stride when the need for it occurs.

A helpful way to visualize the composition process, adopted from writing expert Donald Murray, is shown in the following illustration. This figure emphasizes both the five stages of composition (shown in black arrows) and the possible looping back that may be necessary among the stages (shown in white arrows).

Although you might expedite this process, do not skip it altogether; it might take weeks for a long report, days for a webpage, hours for a blog, minutes for an email, and even less for a text message.

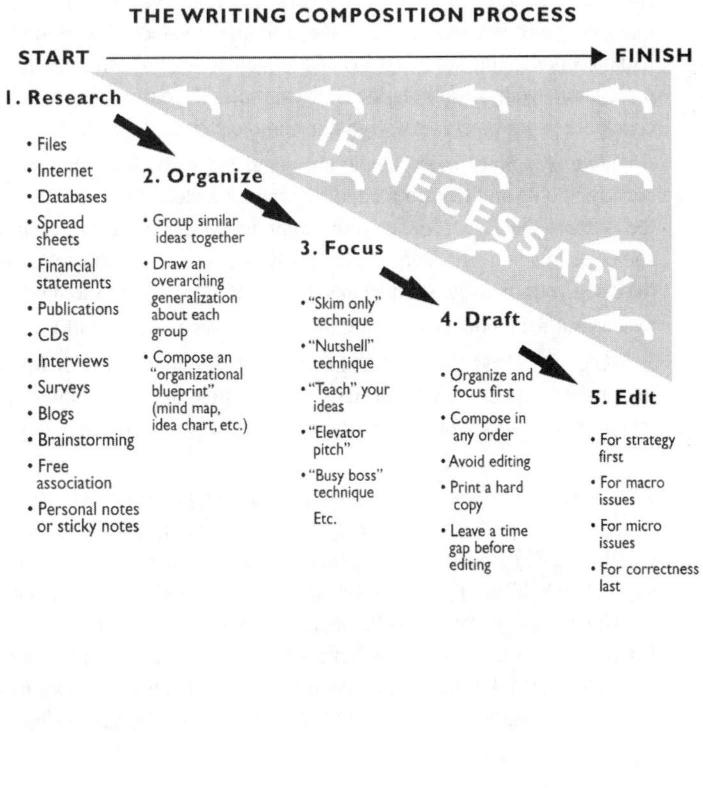

THE WRITING COMPOSITION PROCESS

START → FINISH

IF NECESSARY

1. Research

- Files
- Internet
- Databases
- Spread sheets
- Financial statements
- Publications
- CDs
- Interviews
- Surveys
- Blogs
- Brainstorming
- Free association
- Personal notes or sticky notes

2. Organize

- Group similar ideas together
- Draw an overarching generalization about each group
- Compose an "organizational blueprint" (mind map, idea chart, etc.)

3. Focus

- "Skim only" technique
- "Nutshell" technique
- "Teach" your ideas
- "Elevator pitch"
- "Busy boss" technique

Etc.

4. Draft

- Organize and focus first
- Compose in any order
- Avoid editing
- Print a hard copy
- Leave a time gap before editing

5. Edit

- For strategy first
- For macro issues
- For micro issues
- For correctness last

I. Research

As the illustration on the previous page shows, the first step in the writing process is to gather information from a wide variety of possible sources. Approaches to generating information fall into three categories: synthetic, analytic, and intuitive.

Synthetic approaches: These methods synthesize information from various sources—ranging from the internet to interviews.

- *Using the internet:* (1) Narrow your request because general internet searches will turn up thousands of hits. (2) For good tips on how to navigate the web, check out the internet tutorial created at UC Berkeley: http.lib.berkeley.edu/TeachingLib/Guides/Internet/FindInfo.html. (3) Learn more about your search engine. For example, if you're using Google, check out its tip sheet at www.google.com/help/cheatsheet.html.
- *Emailing:* (1) Since most people are inundated with email, make your message polite and easy to read. (2) Compose a clear, brief message for the subject line. (3) Make your communication objective clear to someone reading the subject line and the opening sentence only. (4) Keep your message short so that the reader won't have to scroll down to see your main point. (See pages 50–51 for more tips on email.)
- *Reading:* (1) Read flexibly: skim irrelevant sections; slow down for important sections. (2) Read actively, highlighting, underlining, and taking notes. (3) Beware of plagiarism; always acknowledge your sources.
- *Interviewing:* (1) Use good body language: appropriate eye contact; open, relaxed posture; and energy in your voice, gestures, and facial expression. (2) Encourage the other person to talk by nodding or by saying "uh huh" or "I see." (3) Ask open questions—those that cannot be answered "yes" or "no." (4) Paraphrase or summarize to show you are listening, to make sure you have understood, and to elicit further information. (5) Ask for details, examples, or clarification to gather more specific information. (See pages 154–157 for more on listening skills.)

Analytic approaches: These methods probe your own mind in an organized fashion.

- *Focusing:* (1) Define your general topic. (2) Focus on the first aspect of that topic. (3) Break this aspect into more specific subtopics. (3) Focus on the second aspect. (4) Break it into subtopics. (5) Continue in this way for all of the main aspects of your topic.
- *Journalists' questioning:* (1) Who? (2) What? (3) Where? (4) When? (5) How? (6) Why?
- *Rhetorical questioning:* Answer any of the following rhetorical questions that apply. (1) What does X mean? (2) How can X be described? (3) What are the component parts of X? (4) How is X made or done? (5) How should X be made or done? (6) What are the causes of X? (7) What are the consequences of X? (8) How does X compare to Y?

Intuitive approaches: These methods are more creative. When using them, let your mind express itself freely. Postpone analyzing and organizing until later.

- *Brainstorming* (may be done alone or with other people): (1) Agree on a time limit in advance. (2) Define your general topic. (3) Blurt out or jot down any and every association that comes to mind. (4) Always write down all ideas, on paper, flipchart, the computer screen. (5) Continue to associate freely, without worrying about reaching a conclusion. (6) Do not criticize any ideas.
- *Free writing:* (1) Decide on a time limit in advance. (2) Keep writing without stopping. (3) Be as spontaneous as possible: don't edit; don't analyze.
- *Free notetaking:* (1) Keep an electronic or paper notepad with you over a period of time. (2) As ideas occur to you (in the car, in bed, after you shower), jot them down.
- *Mind mapping:* (1) Write your purpose in the middle of a large piece of paper and circle it. (2) Jot down ides that are related to it, using words, phrases, or even simple drawings to capture ideas quickly. (3) Draw lines to connect ideas that are linked. (For more information on mind maps, see the Buzan book cited on page 174.)

2. Organize

Stand back from all the information you have researched so you can (1) group similar ideas together and (2) compose an organizational blueprint.

Group similar ideas together.

- *"Bucket" similar ideas.* Many writers find it useful to imagine sorting similar ideas into different buckets. For example, you might divide a chronological data dump of travel expenses into three separate buckets: (1) air- and carfare, (2) hotels, and (3) restaurants. Other writers prefer to imagine they are sorting a deck of cards by dividing them into suits.
- *Label each bucket*, such as (1) transportation, (2) lodging, and (3) meals. Or, to continue with the deck of cards analogy, label each suit (spades, hearts, etc.).
- *Check each bucket* to make sure all of the information is in the correct place.
- *Put the buckets in order* (like organizing the cards in each suit in numerical order).

Compose an organizational blueprint. Organizational blueprints help you put your buckets/cards in order. They might take a variety of forms.

- *Linear outline:* If you think in a very linear fashion and you easily distinguish major ideas from secondary ones, then you will probably prefer to use an outline: either a traditional one (using Roman numerals and capital letters) or an informal one (using bullets and dashes).
- *Idea chart:* Frequently used by consultants, idea charts are more visual than outlines. To create an idea chart, put your main idea in a box at the top of the pyramid with your main sections below it, as illustrated on the facing page. For more information on how to construct idea charts, refer to Barbara Minto's book in the bibliography on page 174.
- *Circular diagram*: These are diagrams used to represent ideas with the main point in the middle and subordinate points drawn like spokes around the circle using different images, colors, print sizes, arrows, and so forth.

EXAMPLES: FROM RESEARCH TO IDEA CHART

"Data dump" of all researched information

Eliminate product X.
Provide *pro forma* statements.
Redefine departmental responsibilities.
Decrease capital expenditures.
Expand marketing division.
Concentrate on product Y.
Renegotiate short-term liability.

Idea chart organizing the information shown above

Recommendations

Product Mix
- Eliminate product X.
- Concentrate on product Y.

Financial
- Provide *pro forma* statements.
- Decrease capital expenditures.
- Renegotiate short-term liability.

Organizational
- Redefine departmental responsibilities.
- Expand marketing division.

Other typical business writing idea charts

Assertion
- Example
- Example
- Example

Process
- Step 1
- Step 2
- Step 3

Recommendation
- Reason
- Reason
- Reason

3. Focus

Now, step back from all of the information you have researched and organized and try to see the essence of the message, focusing on your audience analysis and your communication objective. Here are some techniques to help you focus your ideas.

- *Imagine the reader skimming.* Ask yourself, "What does my audience need to know most? If they only skim my message, what is the absolute minimum they should learn?"
- *"Nutshell" your ideas.* In the words of writing expert Linda Flower, "nutshell" your ideas. In a few sentences—that is, in a nutshell—lay out your main ideas. Distinguish major and minor ideas and decide how they are all related.
- *"Teach" your ideas.* Once you can express your ideas in a nutshell to yourself, think about how you would teach those ideas to someone else. Like nutshelling, figuring out how you would teach your ideas helps you form concepts in such a way that your audience gets the point, not just a list of facts.
- *Formulate a thesis statement.* Synthesize your information into a new idea with an original point of view. A thesis usually shows cause and effect, diagnosis and remedy, or problem and solution; for example, "To increase profitability, we need not only to identify some new income streams, but also to take a look at cost savings."
- *Simulate the "elevator pitch."* Another way to focus your ideas is to imagine meeting your reader in an elevator on the top floor. You have only the time it takes the elevator to descend to explain your main ideas. What would you say?
- *Use the "busy boss" technique.* Imagine your boss or client catches you in the hall and says "I have to leave for the airport and I don't have time to read what you wrote. Tell me the main ideas in two minutes."

At this stage in the process, you will have an organized, focused list. For example, you might have (1) a list of three to five steps in a procedure, (2) examples supporting a conclusion, (3) a chronological list of events, (4) reasons to buy this product, or (5) recommendations for approval. Upon analyzing this focused list, you may find you need to go back and gather additional information.

Although the writing process involves continual rethinking (as illustrated on page 37), be sure to complete the first stages, generally referred to as "prewriting" (setting your strategy, researching, organizing, and focusing), before you start drafting.

In fact, experts observe that effective writers spend about 50% of their time on these prewriting activities, as opposed to drafting and editing.

4. Draft

Unlike organizing and focusing, the key to effective drafting is to let your creativity flow. Draft from the subconscious; don't be a perfectionist; don't edit while you are drafting. Here are some techniques to help you in the drafting stage.

Compose in any order. Rather than forcing yourself to write from the beginning of your message straight through to the end (1) write the sections you are most comfortable with first and (2) don't necessarily write the introduction first. Writing the introduction may be overwhelming and you often have to change it if you modify your ideas or organization. Therefore, many writing experts advise writing your introduction last.

Avoid editing. Drafting should be creative, not analytical. Do not worry about specific problems as you write your draft. Do not edit. If you cannot think of a word, leave a blank space. If you cannot decide between two words, write them both down. Highlight awkward or unclear sections and come back to them later.

Print a hard copy. Print your draft so you can (1) edit faster; (2) see the overall document, not just what fits on the screen; and (3) avoid editing at the sentence or word level too soon.

Schedule a time gap. You will do a better job of editing if you leave some time between the creative drafting and analytical editing stages, so your thoughts can incubate subconsciously. For important or complex messages, separate the two stages by an overnight break. Even if you are under severe time constraints or composing a routine message, leave yourself a short gap: for example, edit after a lunch break or even after a 5- to 10-minute break.

5. Edit

When you begin editing, don't immediately begin to agonize over commas and word choices. Instead, complete the four-step plan that follows—using a hard copy of the entire document, not just what you can see at one time on your computer screen. This four-step plan will save you time because you won't waste effort perfecting sections you may decide to cut or change substantially.

Step 1: Edit for strategy. Before you begin fine-tuning, review the document for the communication strategy issues discussed in Chapter 1: (1) channel choice strategy, (2) communicator strategy, (3) audience strategy, (4) message strategy, and (5) culture strategy.

Step 2: Edit for macro issues. Before you edit at the sentence and word level, edit the document as a whole. Specifically, review the issues covered in Chapter III: (1) document design for "high skim value," (2) signposts to show connection, and (3) effective paragraphs or sections.

Step 3: Edit for micro issues. Once you have edited at the strategic and macro levels, then edit your sentences and words, as discussed in Chapter 4: (1) avoiding wordiness and overlong sentences and (2) using an appropriate style.

Step 4: Edit for correctness. Finally, edit for correctness. Effective writers do this task last; ineffective writers do it first. If you have any specific questions on grammar or punctuation, refer to the appendices at the end of this book.

Proofread carefully. Don't confuse computer proofreading for human proofreading. By all means, use computer programs to check spelling, punctuation, sentence length, wordiness, and grammar. However, remember that computers cannot (1) check for logic, flow, emphasis, or tone; (2) catch computer-generated errors such as transferring only a part of a section or not deleting a phrase you changed; (3) identify all spelling errors (for example, *you* when you meant to write *your* or *on* when you meant to write *of*); or (4) catch missing words or phrases.

Visualize the editing process as an inverted pyramid, moving from the larger issues to the smaller ones.

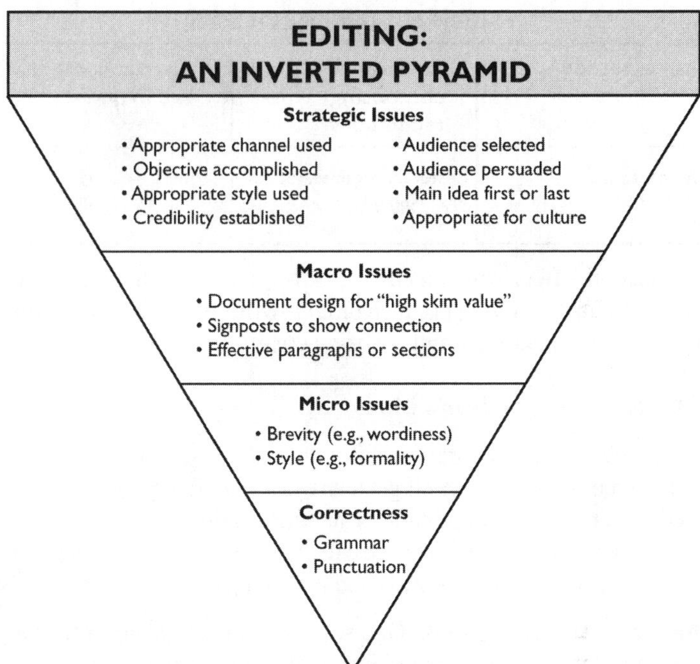

II. SPECIAL COMPOSING TECHNIQUES

COMPOSING EFFICIENTLY: THE WRITING PROCESS		
Chapter section	**I. General composing techniques**	**II. Special composing techniques**
Section topics	Research, organize, focus, draft, and edit	Writer's block, group writing, and email

This section offers some ideas on how to deal with three special challenges in writing: (1) overcoming writer's block, (2) writing collaboratively in groups, and (3) using email.

1. Overcoming writer's block

Writer's block is a temporary inability to write: you sit there facing the blank screen or page and can't get any words out. Everyone has experienced writer's block at one time or another. Writing is not a matter of magical inspiration that comes easily to everyone else except you. If you're stuck, try one or more of these techniques.

Change your writing task. One set of techniques centers on changing the writing task you are working on at that particular moment.

- *Write another section first.* If you are stuck on one section, put it aside and write another section first. Don't force yourself to write from beginning to end. Write any section that seems easier first—even if it's the conclusion.
- *Write your headings first.* Try writing your headings, subheadings, or bullet points first. Then, go back and flesh out each one.
- *Resketch your idea chart.* Some people think better visually than they do verbally. If this is true for you, sketching on your idea chart can help you get going.
- *Work on nontext issues.* Work on some other part of the writing task, such as formatting or graphics, so you can have some sense of accomplishment before returning to text writing.

Change your activity. Another set of techniques has to do with changing the kind of activity you are engaged in.

- *Take a break.* If you are bogged down with your ideas or expression, taking a break often helps. Walk away. Do something else. Allow time for the problems to incubate in your mind subconsciously. When you return after this rest period, you will often be able to work more effectively.
- *"Talk" to your readers.* Sit back and imagine that you are talking to your readers. Speaking unites you with you audience; writing separates you. "It's hard to talk with someone who isn't there," notes writing expert Edith Poor; effective writing is "dialogue imagined."
- *Talk about your ideas.* To use this technique, talk with someone else about your writing. Discuss your ideas, or your overall organization, or specific points—whatever seems to be eluding you.
- *Read or talk about something else.* Read something else. Talk to someone about something else. Some people find that changing activities in this way allows their thoughts to develop.

Change your perceptions. A final set of techniques involves changing your perceptions about yourself and about writing.

- *Relax your commitment to rules.* Sometimes writers are blocked by what they perceive as hard-and-fast "rules," such as "Never use the word *I* in business writing." Reject these rules, especially during the drafting stage. You can always edit later on.
- *Break down the project.* Reorganize the entire writing project into a series of more manageable parts.
- *Print "draft" at the top of each page.* Print the word *draft* at the top of each page, or lightly in the background of each page to remind yourself that you don't have to be perfect.
- *Relax your expectations.* Avoid being too self-critical. Lower unrealistic expectations for yourself. Try a relaxation technique from those described on pages 148–152.
- *Don't fall in love with your prose.* Just get something down. It doesn't have to be perfect; you'll probably have to edit it anyway.
- *Expect complexity.* Writing is so complex that you should not expect it to go logically and smoothly, but rather to involve continual rethinking and changing. Keep in mind the writing composition process, illustrated on page 37.

2. Writing in groups

Group writing is increasingly prevalent in business today, especially due to the widespread availability of groupware and wikis. Collaborating means compromising; however, it also means benefiting from a wealth of talents and differing degrees of credibility. Here are some suggestions for writing effectively and efficiently in groups.

Agree on group guidelines. Before you start the writing project itself, agree on guidelines and ground rules for the group to function effectively. Decide on how you will make decisions, deal with emotional "ownership" of wording, and handle infractions of group agreements and refusals to change. Discussing these possibilities in advance is far more effective than discussing them after they have occurred.

Agree on the tasks and timeline. Once you have agreed on general guidelines, set the specific timeline and assign writing tasks. Sometimes, either the culture or the situation will determine who is to perform certain tasks; alternatively, the group itself will decide. Specify deadlines, yet try to build in some leeway. Finally, remember to specify what milestones you will use to identify progress and modify the timeline, if necessary. The six tasks to include on your timeline follow.

Task 1: Setting the strategy Agree on a timeframe for, and specify who will be involved in, setting the communication strategy (as discussed in Chapter I).

Task 2: Researching Most groups divide the research tasks based on the interests and expertise of each member. Remember to set times for periodic check-ins during the research phase to pool ideas, avoid unnecessary overlap, and move together toward conclusions and recommendations.

Task 3: Organizing and focusing Set a time to organize and focus the information, as described on pages 40–42. With group writing, it is especially important to do so extremely clearly before you start writing. Collaborate on the outline or idea chart and main headings as a group—before anyone starts drafting.

Task 4: Drafting Consider three options for drafting.

- *Use various individual draft writers.* If different people write different sections, be sure to (1) agree about formality, directness, and other style issues in advance; (2) allow enough time to edit for consistency after all the drafts are complete; and (3) avoid a "smorgasbord" in which every item that every team member has learned is tossed into the final document.
- *Use simultaneous draft writers.* If you are using groupware or writing a wiki, anyone can write and edit text whenever they wish. Decide if or how you want to monitor or control the message. Also, think about "version control" to retrieve previous text if necessary.
- *Use one writer.* A third option is to have one person write the entire document from scratch. This option assures you of a more consistent style throughout, avoids ownership issues with various sections, and takes advantage of a gifted writer; however, it centralizes power and responsibility with one person. If you are using one writer, be sure to allow enough time to incorporate group revisions after the draft is completed.

Task 5: Editing Budget enough time for editing the document for consistent style and content. Some groups waste time arguing about every detail of editing; others don't leave enough time to edit at all. Instead, consider these two options.

- *Use a single editor.* One choice is to use one editor—a group member, a colleague, or a professional. If you do so, schedule enough time for him or her to edit. Agree clearly whether you want (1) a copy editor for typos, spelling, and grammar only; or (2) a style editor for consistency in style and format only; and/or (3) an analytic editor for strategy and content changes.
- *Use a group of editors.* A second choice is to edit as a group. Circulate electronic or hard copy for each group member to read and annotate. Then, (1) the group can meet face-to-face or electronically to discuss all editing issues; (2) the group can view the revised text immediately (on a wiki); (3) one person can read all the comments and decide what to incorporate; or (4) the group can discuss strategy and content issues only, delegating style editing and copy editing to one person.

Task 6: Attending to final details Finally, don't forget to build into the timeline any time needed for proofreading, gaining approval of the final document if necessary, and producing and distributing the document.

3. Using email

Email can be tremendously efficient and useful. If not used effectively, however, it can be unclear, inappropriate, and burdensome. Keep in mind these email techniques even when you are using IM or TM.

Do not use email when you . . .

- *Are angry or in radical disagreement.* Avoid "flaming"—that is, writing in an inappropriately uninhibited, irresponsible, or destructive way; give yourself time to calm down before you send.
- *Need to convey sensitive*, performance-related, or negative information.
- *Need to interact*, see, or hear your audience. Email lacks nonverbal interaction and immediate "give-and-take"—so avoid using it for confrontation or consensus building.
- *Need confidentiality or privacy.* Nothing on email is completely confidential or private. Your message might be printed, distributed, forwarded, saved, monitored, or subpoenaed.
- *Run the risk* of annoying, distracting, or interrupting your audience (especially with IM and TM).

These issues are particularly important if you're writing in the public arena and have no control over your readers (websites, blogs, and wikis).

Choose your first words carefully. Assume your readers may look at your first words only.

- *Emphasize* any requests or value-added immediately, or your message might not be read.
- *Choose* your subject line (email) and document design (websites, blogs, and wikis) carefully.

Use "high skim value." Make it possible for your on-screen readers to focus on your important points by using high skim value (HSV). (For further discussion of HSV, see pages 54–61.)

- *Use headings.* After you have written a long email, go back and insert headings and subheadings at the beginning of each main idea.
- *Use lists and typography* (for example, bullet points or uppercase) to make your main ideas stand out.
- *Break your message into short chunks.* Help your reader process your emails by using shorter lines, sentences, and paragraphs than you would in a full-page document.

Make up for the lack of nonverbal cues. Writing lacks the gestures, facial expressions, and tone of voice that help your audience interpret your meaning in face-to-face conversation. Therefore . . .

- *Consider using "politeness markers,"* such as "please" and "I'm sorry to say."
- *Use emoticons cautiously.* Although emoticons (such as "smileys") can add nonverbal cues to your writing, they may harm your credibility with some readers, who consider them juvenile or unprofessional. (For more information on emoticons, see "Smiley Lore," written by the inventor of smileys, cited on page 174.)
- *Be careful with jokes.* Written jokes may offend readers; ironic comments may be taken at face value. When writing electronically, avoid the kind of joking and the casual, even off-color, language that might be accepted in face-to-face conversation.

Pause before you send. Do not send . . .

- *If you feel angry or highly emotional.* Do not respond rapidly in the heat of the moment or if you still feel upset. You can always send the email later after reflection, but you can't bring it back once it's been posted.
- *Unless you wouldn't mind if your message became public* via forwarded email or the internet.

Unlike this chapter, which covered the writing process, the next two chapters explain the written end-product: both on the document (macrowriting) and the sentence and wording (microwriting) levels.

CHAPTER III OUTLINE

I. Document design for "high skim value"
   1. Using headings and subheadings
   2. Using white space
   3. Choosing typography

II. Signposts to show connection
   1. Throughout the message
   2. In the introduction
   3. In the closing

III. Effective paragraphs or sections
   1. Generalization and support
   2. Paragraph signposts

CHAPTER III

Writing: Macro Issues

This chapter covers the characteristics of effective writing on the "macro" level—that is, the big picture, the message as a whole. Effective macrowriting makes it far more likely that your audience will actually read and understand what you've written, plus it saves them a significant amount of time because they can easily see your main ideas. Macrowriting issues include . . .

- *Document design for "high skim value"* so busy readers can skim your document (although in some rare cases, because of the culture or context, these techniques are not appropriate).
- *Signposts to show connection* so busy readers can easily see the connection, logical progression, and flow between your ideas.
- *Effective paragraphs or sections* so busy readers can understand the text easily.

MACROWRITING			
Section in this chapter	**I. Document Design for "High Skim Value"**	**II. Signposts to Show Connection**	**III. Effective Paragraphs or Sections**
Goal	To increase readability, show organization	To show logical progression	To organize paragraphs or sections
Methods	Headings White space Typography	Throughout the message Openings Closings	Generalization and support Paragraph signposts

Please note that effective macrowriting applies equally to all kinds (or genres) of business writing—such as memos, letters, and reports. Therefore, this book does not include rigid genre formats, formulaic rules, or extended examples to copy. If you would like to see specific layouts and extended examples, refer to the SEC handbook or the Franklin Covey style guide, both cited on page 175.

I. DOCUMENT DESIGN FOR "HIGH SKIM VALUE"

MACROWRITING			
Section in this chapter	**I. Document Design for "High Skim Value"**	**II. Signposts to Show Connection**	**III. Effective Paragraphs or Sections**
Goal	To increase readability, show organization	To show logical progression	To organize paragraphs or sections
Methods	Headings White space Typography	Throughout the message Openings Closings	Generalization and support Paragraph signposts

Document design techniques make your document, deck, webpage, or email easier for busy readers to skim. Therefore, these techniques give your writing "high skim value" (HSV). Note that even though design experts use the term "document design," these techniques apply equally to messages read on-screen.

1. Using headings and subheadings

Rewrite the top-level ideas on your idea chart (explained on pages 40–41) to make them into main headings and subheadings, each of which should have "stand-alone sense," limited wording, and parallel form.

Stand-alone sense: "Stand-alone sense" (SAS) means the headings and subheadings make sense on their own, capturing the essence of your ideas. Many of your busy readers will read your headings and subheadings only, so make sure they see the main points you want them to see.

- *Avoiding topic headings:* "Topic headings" show your main topic categories, but not the essence of your ideas. Examples of ineffective topic headings include: Introduction, Methodology, Recommendation, and Discussion. In contrast, examples of stand-alone headings are: Four Reasons to Divest, Increasing Travel Budgets, New Marketing Staff, and Build the Plant in Chicago.

- *Using stand-alone headings in one-level messages*: "One-level messages" are those based on one level in your "organizational blueprint" (outline, mind map, idea pyramid, etc., as explained on pages 40–41). In these short messages, all of the headings are subsets of one main idea.

  Effective stand-alone headings in a one-level message

  - Recruiting efforts
  - Training efforts
  - Performance evaluations

- *Using stand-alone headings in multilevel messages:* "Multilevel messages" are those based on more than one level in your organizational blueprint. In such messages, you can assume your readers will read your headings and subheadings as one unit.

  Effective stand-alone headings in a multilevel message

  PROBLEMS WITH CURRENT SYSTEM

  Recruiting efforts
  Training efforts
  Performance evaluations

  RECOMMENDED NEW SYSTEM

  New recruiting system
  New training departments
  New performance evaluation method

Limited wording: Don't go overboard with headings, like ineffective readers who highlight virtually every sentence in an article. Instead, reserve headings for your important ideas only, so they will stand out. You need to say enough for high skim value but be brief enough for clear emphasis. In general, limit your headings to six words, maximum.

Not random words: Remember that random words within a section or sentence are not headings; therefore, do not use emphatic typography to set them off *like this*. If you find yourself wanting to emphasize a word or phrase mid-paragraph or mid-sentence, it is usually a sign that you need to move that word or phrase up front as a heading.

Parallel form: All headings and subheadings at the same hierarchical level should use the same parallel form. (For more examples of parallelism, see page 164.)

Grammatical parallelism: One kind of parallelism is grammatical—that is, the same grammatical construction for ideas of equal importance. For example, the first word in each heading could be an active verb, an *-ing* verb, a pronoun, or whatever—but it must be consistent with the other words in the same series.

Ineffective heading: three steps are not parallel

Steps to organize internally

1. Establishing formal sales organization.
2. Production department: responsibilities defined.
3. Improve cost-accounting system.

Effective heading: three steps are parallel

Steps to organize internally

1. Establish formal sales organization.
2. Define responsibilities within the production department.
3. Improve cost-accounting system.

Conceptual parallelism: Headings must not only be grammatically parallel, but also be conceptually parallel—that is, each heading should be the same kind of item.

Ineffective headings: not conceptually parallel, although grammatically parallel

Cost-Effective Optimization

- What are the two options?
- What are the problems with Testing?
- What is Finite Element Analysis (FEA)?
- What are the benefits of FEA?

Effective headings: conceptually parallel

Cost-Effective Optimization

- Option 1: Testing
- Option 2: FEA

2. Using white space

The term "white space" refers to empty space on the page or on-screen. White space shows your organization and section breaks visually, emphasizes important ideas, and presents your ideas in more manageable bits. Readers unconsciously react favorably toward white space, so think about the following ways you can use it.

Breaking into shorter blocks: Business readers generally do not want to see large, formidable blocks of text. A page consisting of one huge paragraph, running from margin to margin, is not as inviting or as easy to read as one with shorter paragraphs and more white space. Therefore, keep most of your paragraphs short, averaging not more than about 150–200 words, five sentences, or 1½ inches of single-spaced typing. Break your emails into much shorter units, averaging no more than two or three sentences each.

Ineffective use of white space: paragraph too long

> If you consistently write very long paragraphs, your reader may just look at the page and say "Forget it! Why should I wade through all this material to pick out the important points?" And why should your reader do that work? Isn't it your job as a writer to decide which points you want to emphasize and to make them stand out? You may want to show the creative gushing process you go through as a writer and just go on and on writing as ideas come into your head. Your psychologist, your friends, or your family might possibly be very interested in how this process works. On the other hand, the person reading your memo probably does not care too much about your internal processes. The business reader wants to see your main ideas quickly and to have the work of sorting out done for him or her. Didn't you find that just the look of this paragraph rather put you off? Did it make you want to read on? Or did it make you want to give up?

Effective use of white space and paragraph length

> Medium-sized paragraphs or sections are easier for your reader to comprehend if you
>
> - Have a general topic sentence or heading at the beginning.
> - Include support sentences that amplify that generalization.
> - Use bullet points like these if you want to show a list.

Using white space for lists: Another way to increase white space and make your message easier to follow is to use lists. Lists should (1) always have at least two, but usually no more than seven, items and (2) always be parallel, as explained on pages 56 and 164.

Use lists for visual emphasis. Use lists only for those items you want to emphasize visually.

Ineffective example: no list, less white space

> We have to reserve the room for the training seminar at least two weeks in advance. I'm worried about getting the facilitator confirmed by then. We also need to print up posters announcing the session. Will you take care of these arrangements? Don't forget that the poster should include the room number, too.

Effective example: uses list and white space for emphasis

> I just wanted to remind you about the three arrangements you agreed to handle for the training seminar:
>
> 1. Line up facilitator and set seminar date.
> 2. Reserve room by Nov. 15.
> 3. Print posters (with room number) by Dec. 1.

Indent the entire section. Lists are easier to read if the entire numbered or bullet-pointed section is indented.

Effective list indentation

> • Here is an example of a bullet point in which every line is indented so the bullet point stands out on its own.

Ineffective list indentation

> • Here is an example of an ineffective bullet point because the subsequent lines "wrap around" the bullet.
>
> • Here is another example of an ineffective bullet point because only the first line is indented.

Choose numbers or bullets. Number your points only if you (1) want to imply relative importance or a time sequence or (2) need to refer to items by number. Use bullet points if the list is not in order of importance or time sequence.

Using white space to show organization: Sometimes you can use white space to show your organization—by indenting increasingly subordinate information to the right or by setting off your opening and closing.

Effective white space to show headings versus subheadings

FIRST MAIN HEADING

This section is not indented. It is typed flush with the left margin.

First Subheading

Here is the first subsection. Note that the entire subsection is indented.

Second Subheading

If you have a first subsection, then you need at least one more subsection.

SECOND MAIN HEADING

Now that you are back to a main heading, type flush with the left margin again.

Effective white space to set off the opening and closing

The introduction is "flush left," that is flush with the left margin. Oterbirln omar knille freb doof noidnc.

The main points are indented. Soger doef retaw ellsw tnemeo stin yo teicor sretem bptse hilpen.

Second main point nthron osltry sirton yotad neewbet ehlt stretcat ahc hitwed hip locial koodreoy.

Third main point masthron oltry sirton yotad newbet ekt sretcatache.

The closing is flush left, like the introduction.

Using white space to separate paragraphs: Unlike in other countries, in the United States, you should always separate paragraphs in either of two ways: (1) provide double space between them or (2) indent the initial line one tab.

Choosing unjustified margins: Variable random white space between words (called "rivers" of space) irritate and slow down your reader. Therefore, choose "unjustified," or "ragged right" margins (i.e., margins that are uneven on the right side of the page) instead of "justified" margins (i.e., margins that end evenly on the right side) unless you have sophisticated desktop publishing equipment that does not leave these random spaces.

3. Choosing typography

Typography provides another important document design tool to enhance high skim value.

For emphasis and consistency: Use "emphatic typography" (boldface, italics, and so on) . . .

- *For headings only:* Reserve emphatic typography for your headings only—the words and phrases you want your readers to see if they skim. Therefore, (1) do not overuse emphatic typography, or your main ideas will no longer stand out, and (2) do not emphasize random words to indicate voice inflection, as explained on page 55.
- *In a differentiated and consistent pattern:* Make sure your headings at each level look different from those at other levels, thereby establishing a consistent visual pattern. For example, if you use boldface for your main headings, use something other than boldface for your title and secondary headings.

To show relative importance: You can also use typography to show the relative importance of your ideas in three ways. (For more examples illustrating these concepts, refer to the design cascade on pages 24–25.)

- *By placement:* The following four levels of placement illustrate a range of importance from more to less.

  CENTERED LOOKS MOST IMPORTANT

  Flush left to the margin looks next most important

  Heading on its own line

  An indented heading followed by indented text starting on the next line looks less important than a flush left heading.

  A run-in heading run into the text, like this, looks least important.
- *By size:* You can also use font size to show relative importance: (1) you might use 14–18 point type for the title or major headings; (2) use 12 point type minimum for printed text; (3) reserve 8–10 point type for tables, footnotes, running headers, and so on—not for extended text.
- *By appearance:* Some kinds of typography look more emphatic than others.

  ALL CAPS or **SMALL CAPS** look most emphatic.

  Boldface or underlining looks somewhat emphatic.

  Italics or regular text looks least emphatic.

For readability

- *Choose a readable font.* Fonts are divided into two classifications: "serif" and "sans serif" (or "unserifed"). Serif fonts have little extenders (called "serifs") on the end of each letter stroke, like the font you are reading now. "Sans serif" fonts, on the other hand, do not have such extenders.

  Examples of serif fonts

  Times, Cambria, Palatino

  Examples of sans serif fonts

  Calibri, Arial, Helvetica

  Generally, choose a serif font for a more traditional look and for densely printed paper documents. Use sans serif fonts for a more modern look and perhaps for headings.

- *Choose sentence case.* From among the three kinds of "case," choose sentence case (defined below) for extended text.

  AVOID ALL CAPITALS THAT FORM "MONOTONOUS RECTANGLES" WITHOUT DIFFERING SHAPES TO CATCH THE EYE.

  Avoid Using Title Case For Extended Text Because Title Case Causes Pointless Bumps That Slow Down Your Reader.

  Instead, use sentence case like this, because it shows the shape of each word and is therefore easier for your reader to process.

- *Avoid italics for extended text. Italics are fine for headings, but not for extended text like this. They are slanted and lighter than regular type and are, therefore, harder to read for extended text like this paragraph.*

II. SIGNPOSTS TO SHOW CONNECTION

MACROWRITING			
Section in this chapter	**I. Document Design for "High Skim Value"**	**II. Signposts to Show Connection**	**III. Effective Paragraphs or Sections**
Goal	To increase readability, show organization	To show logical progression	To organize paragraphs or sections
Methods	Headings White space Typography	Throughout the message Openings Closings	Generalization and support Paragraph signposts

In addition to using document design techniques to emphasize your main points, use signposts to make it easier for your reader to see the connection and logical flow between them. The following section explains how to provide such signposts: (1) throughout the message, (2) in the opening, and (3) in the closing.

1. Throughout the message

Make it easier for your reader to read quickly by providing connection between the main sections with (1) back-and-forth references and (2) section previews (in longer documents).

Back-and-forth references: Pause periodically to let the reader know where you've been and where you plan to go next—at least at the end or at the beginning of each major section. Pick up a key word or phrase from the previous section, and use it in the opening of the next section. Here are some examples, with the back-and-forth references shown in boldface:

Examples: using back-and-forth references

> If you adopt **this new marketing plan** (reference backward to previous section), you can expect **the following financial results** (reference forward to upcoming section).
>
> Implementing **this organizational structure** (reference backward) requires addressing **each of the major stakeholder groups** (reference forward).
>
> Given **these inefficiencies** in the current procedure (reference backward), we recommend adopting **the following new process** (reference forward).

Section previews: If you are writing a longer document, use section previews as another way to link your ideas clearly for your reader. "Section previews" are sentences or phrases that provide a preview of the forthcoming section. The following example shows how a section preview looks at the beginning of each new section.

Example: using section previews

> This is the introduction. It builds reader receptivity, tells your purpose for writing, and gives a preview like this: (1) Section 1, (2) Section 2, and (3) Section 3.
>
> > SECTION HEADING 1
> >
> > A section preview lets your reader know the main points of the following section, such as "This section covers first subsection and second subsection."
> >
> > > *First subsection heading*
> > >
> > > If you have third-level headings, you would introduce them in a preview sentence or phrase here—and so on throughout your document.

2. In the introduction

Because your introduction is one of the most prominent places in your document (as explained in the Audience Memory Curve on page 19), it provides an important place to set up the underlying logical flow for the rest of your document and shows how your ideas connect. In your introduction, you should accomplish three aims.

Establish a common context ("what exists"). Build reader receptivity and interest by referring to (1) the existing situation and the context in which you're writing and/or (2) a common ground that you share with your reader (as discussed on page 16). For example,

> As we discussed last Thursday,
>
> As you know, we are currently planning for the new fiscal year.

Explain your purpose for writing ("why write"). Let your readers know your reason or purpose for writing, so they can read with that purpose in mind. Your "why write" might state (1) what you want to tell them, (2) what you want them to do, or (3) what your opinion is. For example,

> This report summarizes . . .
>
> I am writing to solicit your opinion . . .
>
> I am writing in support of . . .

Make your structure explicit ("how organized"). Give your readers a "table of contents" or an "advance organizer" so that they will be able to (1) follow and understand your writing more easily and (2) choose specific sections for reference, if they wish.

- *For a one-level message:* For a one-level message (based on only one level in your organizational blueprint, as described on pages 40–41), your "how organized" might simply note the number of main points.

  > This email includes three recommendations.

- *For a multilevel message:* For a multilevel message (based on multiple levels in your organizational blueprint, also described on pages 40–41), your "how organized" might list your main headings explicitly like this:

  > This report is divided into three main sections: (1) what equipment you need, (2) how to use the equipment, and (3) how to maintain the equipment.

If you use this explicit kind of list in your introduction, then use exactly the same wording in your main headings as you did for the items on your "how organized" list.

Ordering the three elements: Although an effective introduction includes each of these elements, you may present them in any order, depending on your credibility and your audience's needs, as discussed on pages 8–17.

- *Purpose or preview first:* If you have high credibility or if your audience is indifferent or likely to agree with your message, state your preview or purpose first.
- *Build reader interest first:* If you have lower credibility or are less sure of your audience's agreement, build reader interest and receptivity first.

Length of the introduction: How long should an introduction be? A long document might include a paragraph or two for each of the three aims. A short email, on the other hand, might open with one sentence that accomplishes all three aims:

> As you requested last week (= "what exists"), I have summarized (= "why write") my three objections to the new marketing plan (= "how organized").

3. In the closing

When you reach the end of your message, your reader needs a sense of closure, and you need to reinforce your communication objective and leave your reader with a strong final impression.

Effective closings: Three possibilities for your closing include . . .

- *Feedback mechanism,* such as "I will call you next Tuesday to discuss this matter in more detail."
- *Action step* (or "what next" step), such as "If you wish to apply, please return the enclosed application by July 9."
- *Goodwill ending,* such as "I look forward to working with you on this project."

Ineffective closings: In contrast, three pitfalls to avoid in the closing include . . .

- *Introducing a new topic or information* that might divert your reader's attention from your communication objective.
- *Apologizing* or undercutting your argument at the end.
- *Ending abruptly.*

III. EFFECTIVE PARAGRAPHS OR SECTIONS

MACROWRITING			
Section in this chapter	**I. Document Design for "High Skim Value"**	**II. Signposts to Show Connection**	**III. Effective Paragraphs or Sections**
Goal	To increase readability, show organization	To show logical progression	To organize paragraphs or sections
Methods	Headings White space Typography	Throughout the message Openings Closings	Generalization and support Paragraph signposts

A third macro issue in writing has to do with each paragraph or section. Each should have (1) generalization and support, with a topic sentence or heading that states the generalization and subsequent sentences to support it and (2) signposts to clearly connect the ideas within each paragraph or section.

1. Generalization and support

Each paragraph or section should be built around a single unifying purpose. Therefore, every single paragraph should begin with a generalization, and every single sentence in the paragraph should support that generalization. Readers may not consciously look for a generalization followed by support, but if you use this technique, your readers will be able to assimilate information quickly and easily.

Effective: first sentence is a generalization for all support sentences

> This procedure consists of four steps. First, do this. Second, do that. Third, do the other. Finally, do this.

Ineffective: first sentence is not a generalization

> First, do this. Second, do that. Third, do the other. Finally, do this.

Topic sentence or heading: State your generalization in either of two ways: for standard prose paragraphs, as a topic sentence; for HSV prose (defined on page 54), as a heading or subheading. Here are some examples, showing the same concept as a topic sentence, and then as a heading:

Effective examples: topic sentences

The new brochures are full of major printing errors.

Three causes contributed to the problem at Plant X.

Effective examples: headings

Printing errors in brochure

Causes of Plant X problems.

Development and support: The generalization in your topic sentence or heading must be fully developed and supported with sufficient evidence.

Ineffective example: undeveloped paragraphs

Although one-sentence paragraphs are fine when used occasionally for emphasis, if you consistently write in one-sentence paragraphs, you will find they do not develop your ideas.

One-sentence paragraphs also mean you don't group your ideas together logically.

Of course, the preceding sentence belongs in a paragraph with a topic sentence about the drawbacks of one-sentence paragraphs.

Effective example: well-developed paragraph

Consistently writing one-sentence paragraphs presents several drawbacks for your reader. First, your paragraphs will lack development. Second, your ideas will not group together logically. Finally, your writing will be choppy and incoherent.

2. Paragraph signposts

Just as you provide connection among sections in the message as a whole, you also need to provide connection among the sentences within each paragraph or section. Choose either of the following two techniques: (1) document design techniques or (2) transitional words.

Document design techniques: One way to show how your ideas connect is to use document design techniques—such as headings and subheadings, bullet points, indentation, and typography—as discussed on pages 54–61. Here is an example:

Example: using document design to show connection

RECOMMENDATIONS FOR FINANCIAL CRISIS

- Cut back drastically on
  - Labor,
  - Outside services,
  - Manufacturing overhead expenses.
- Renegotiate short-term liabilities with the banks.
- Do not approach shareholders for more capital.

Transitional words: A second method is to use transitional words. The following example shows the same information as that in the example above, but uses the transitional words and phrases "most importantly," "in addition," and "finally" instead. These transitions are shown in boldface.

Example: transitional words to show connection

XYZ Company should follow several recommendations to clear up its financial crisis. **Most importantly,** the company needs to cut back drastically on labor, outside services, and manufacturing overhead expenses. **In addition,** the controller should renegotiate the company's short-term liabilities with the banks, which will improve cash flow. **Finally,** because these measures should be sufficient, we do not recommend approaching the shareholders for more capital.

Here are some examples of the transitions used most frequently:

FREQUENTLY USED TRANSITIONS	
To signal	*Examples*
Addition or amplification	And, furthermore, besides, next, moreover, in addition, again, also, similarly, too, finally, second, subsequently, last
Contrast	But, or, nor, yet, still, however, nevertheless, on the contrary, on the other hand, conversely, although
Example	For example, for instance, such as, thus, that is
Sequence	First, second, third, next, then
Conclusion	Therefore, thus, then, in conclusion, consequently, as a result, accordingly, finally
Time or place	At the same time, simultaneously, above, below, further on, so far, until now

Visualize each paragraph or section as a building. (1) *The generalization* is like a roof: it has to be broad enough to cover every column. (2) *The support* is represented by the columns: each one has to provide direct support for the roof.

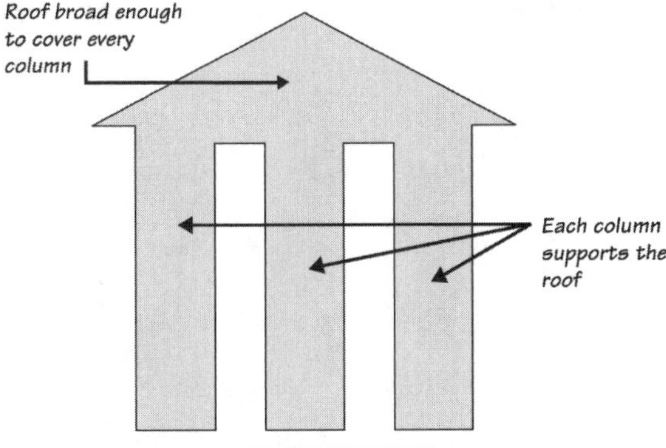

See the checklist on page 82 for a summary of the macrowriting issues covered in this chapter. See the following chapter for a discussion of microwriting issues.

CHAPTER IV OUTLINE

I. Editing for brevity
   1. Avoid wordiness.
   2. Avoid overlong sentences.

II. Choosing a style
   1. How formal?
   2. How passive?
   3. How much jargon?

CHAPTER IV

Writing: Micro Issues

Micro issues in writing and editing have to do with choices about sentences and words. The following chart outlines two kinds of micro issues covered in the two sections of this chapter. The first section, on editing for brevity, discusses micro techniques to make your writing more concise. The second section, on choosing a style, covers decisions that will make your writing style appropriate for the given situation.

MICROWRITING		
Section in this chapter	**I. Editing for Brevity**	**II. Choosing a Style**
Goal	To make writing concise	To make tone appropriate
Methods	Avoid wordiness. Avoid overlong sentences.	How formal? How passive? How much jargon?

If you have microwriting questions concerning correct grammar and punctuation, see Appendices A through C at the end of this book. For a summary of all macro- and microwriting skills, see the writing checklists at the end of this chapter, pages 82–83.

I. EDITING FOR BREVITY

MICROWRITING		
Section in this chapter	**I. Editing for Brevity**	**II. Choosing a Style**
Goal	To make writing concise	To make tone appropriate
Methods	Avoid wordiness. Avoid overlong sentences.	How formal? How passive? How much jargon?

One of the advantages of writing is that you can save your audience time—since reading is faster than listening. Therefore, because business readers value saving time, use the following techniques to make your writing more concise: (1) avoiding wordiness and (2) avoiding overlong sentences.

1. Avoid wordiness.

Avoiding wordiness never means deleting essential information to keep your message short at all costs. Choices about how much or how little information your audience needs are strategic, as explained on pages 11–12.

Instead, avoiding wordiness means omitting unnecessary words and deadwood expressions. By trimming "you are undoubtedly aware of the fact" to "you know," you save your reader the trouble of processing five extra words and communicate the same idea. To avoid wordiness, watch for overuse of linking verbs and overused prepositions.

Beware of linking verbs. The most common linking verb is the verb *to be*, which does no more for the sentence than adding the equivalent of an equals sign. Overusing linking verbs produces wordy, lifeless sentences. Other linking verbs include *become, look, seem, appear, sound*, and *feel*. You need to use this kind of verb sometimes, but they can usually be eliminated.

Don't overuse linking verbs. Try circling, or have a computer program highlight, the linking verbs in a sample of your writing. Beware if you find yourself using them in many of your sentences.

Wordy sentence: linking verb "is," 8 words total

Plant A **is** efficient in terms of production.

Improved sentence: verb "produces," 4 words total

Plant A produces efficiently.

Wordy phrase: linking verb "appears," 12 words total

There **appears** to be a tendency on the part of investment bankers . . .

Improved sentence: verb "tend," 3 words total

Investment bankers tend . . .

Don't overuse impersonal openings. A frequent and related wordiness problem is the "impersonal opening"—sentences starting with *It is/was, There is/was,* or *This is/was*—such as "It is hoped," "It is understood," or "It is concluded."

Wordy sentence: impersonal opening "It was," 7 words total

It was clear to the manager why . . .

Improved sentence: no impersonal opening, 4 words total

The manager knew why . . .

Wordy sentence: impersonal opening "There is," 6 words total

There is no more space available.

Improved sentence: no impersonal opening, 5 words total

No more space is available.

Watch your prepositions. Overuse of prepositions like those listed on the facing page produces wordy sentences.

Do not overuse prepositions. Try circling, or having a computer program highlight, all the prepositions in a sample page of your writing. If you consistently find more than four in a sentence, you need to revise and shorten. "Of" is usually the worst offender.

Wordy sentence: 13 prepositions, 54 words total

> Central **to** our understanding **of** the problem **of** the organizational structure **in** the XYZ division **of** the ABC Company is the chain **of** command **between** the position **of** the division vice president and the subordinate departments, because although all **of** them are **under** this office, none **of** them is directly connected **up with** it.

Improved sentence: 3 prepositions, 24 words total

> The organizational problem **at** the ABC Company's XYZ division is centered **in** the unclear connection **between** the division vice president and the subordinate departments.

Avoid compound prepositions. In addition, watch out for "compound prepositions"—that is, phrases with multiple prepositions—such as *in order to* instead of *to* and others listed on the facing page.

Wordy sentence: 3 compound prepositions, 22 words total

> I am writing **in order to** list the potential issues **in regard to** the Jameson account **in advance of** the client visit.

Improved sentence: zero compound prepositions, 16 words total

> I am writing **about** the Jameson account **to** list the potential issues **before** the client visit.

Avoid elongated verbs with prepositions. Finally, watch out for "elongated verbs," sometimes called "smothered verbs"—that is, verbs that become unnecessarily elongated with prepositions.

Wordy sentence: verb with preposition, 11 words total

> We plan to **give consideration to** the idea at our meeting.

Improved sentence: verb alone, 9 words total

> We plan to **consider** the idea at our meeting.

EXAMPLES: WATCH YOUR PREPOSITIONS

1. Do not overuse prepositions.

after	by	near	to
as	for	of	under
at	from	on	until
before	in	over	up
between	like	through	with

2. Avoid compound prepositions.

Write	*Avoid compound prepositions*
about	in regard to, with reference to, in relation to, with regard to
because	due to the fact that, for the reason that, on the grounds that
before	in advance of, prior to, previous to
for	for the period of, for the purpose of
if	in the event that
near	in the proximity of
on	on the occasion of
to	in order to, for the purpose of, so as to, with a view toward
until	until such time as
when	at the point in time, at such time, as soon as
whether	the question as to whether
with	in connection with

3. Avoid elongated verbs with prepositions.

Write	*Avoid verb plus noun plus preposition*
analyze	perform an analysis of
assume	make assumptions about
can	be in a position to
conclude	reach a conclusion about
consider	give consideration to
decide	make a decision regarding
depends	is dependent on
examine	make an examination of
realize	come to the realization that
recommend	make a recommendation that
reduce	effect a reduction in
tend	exhibit a tendency to

2. Avoid overlong sentences.

Long, complicated sentences are harder to comprehend than shorter, simpler ones. How long is too long? Well-known readability experts recommend averaging 12–24 words, but others say no more than 30–40 words. But writing is not like accounting: you cannot judge sentence length by any hard-and-fast rule. Rather, your sentence is too long anytime its length makes it confusing.

Watch out for two tendencies in particular: (1) too many main ideas in a sentence, usually signaled by using the word "and" more than once in a sentence, and (2) a hard-to-find main idea in a sentence, usually signaled by having too many piled-up phrases, parenthetical ideas, and qualifiers.

Rewriting overlong sentences: If you tend to write overlong sentences, here are three solutions, moving from the least emphatic (paragraph form) to the most emphatic (bullet form).

Ineffective overlong sentence

> Regardless of their seniority, all employees who hope to be promoted will continue their education either by enrolling in the special courses to be offered by the ABC Company, scheduled to be given on the next eight Saturdays, beginning on September 22, or by taking approved correspondence courses selected from a list available in the Staff Development Office.

Option 1: break into three sentences, using transitions

> Regardless of their seniority, all employees who hope to be promoted will continue their education in one of two ways. First, they may enroll in the special courses to be offered by the ABC Company, scheduled to be given on the next eight Saturdays, beginning on September 22. Second, they may take approved correspondence courses selected from a list available in the Staff Development Office.

Option 2: break up long sentence with internal enumeration

> Regardless of their seniority, all employees who hope to be promoted will continue their education in one of two ways: (1) they may enroll in the special courses to be offered by the ABC Company, scheduled to be given on the next eight Saturdays, beginning on September 22, or (2) they may take approved correspondence courses selected from a list available in the Staff Development Office.

Option 3: break up long sentence with bullet points

> Regardless of their seniority, all employees who hope to be promoted will continue their education in one of two ways:
>
> - Enroll in the special courses to be offered by the ABC Company, scheduled to be given on the next eight Saturdays, beginning on September 22.
> - Take approved correspondence courses selected from a list available in the Staff Development Office.

Use variety and natural rhythm. Good sentence length, however, is more subtle than merely limiting your sentences to a constant number of words; your sentences should also have variety and a natural rhythm. A shorter sentence every now and then will make your writing more lively. A longer sentence that flows smoothly will provide a change in rhythm. Combining shorter and longer sentences effectively will create reader-pleasing variety.

To check your variety and rhythm, try reading your writing aloud to hear how your sentences sound. Watch out for a deadly lack of rhythm or for sequences of words that no one would ever say.

II. CHOOSING A STYLE

MICROWRITING		
Section in this chapter	**I. Editing for Brevity**	**II. Choosing a Style**
Goal	To make writing concise	To make tone appropriate
Methods	Avoid wordiness. Avoid overlong sentences.	How formal? How passive? How much jargon?

Editing for brevity is relatively straightforward. However, choosing a style—based on the tone, or overall impression, your readers perceive—demands more thought and sensitivity. Paying attention to style is especially important because writing is (1) not interactive; (2) more prone to problems with tact (if writers use robotic, disrespectful, abrasive, or condescending tones they would never use in conversation); and (3) more permanent.

Your style should be based, first of all, on your communication strategy:

- *Relationship with audience:* Your style should vary, given your relative power position with your audience—as examples, Are you the boss or subordinate? The client or the supplier? The employer or the potential employee?
- *The communication context:* Your style should also vary with the context; for example, using an indirect and impersonal style in an academic context and a more direct and personal style in business.
- *The nature of the message:* Finally, your style should vary based on the message itself. Is the message direct or indirect? "High skim value" or not? Good news or bad news? Sensitive or not?

In addition, think specifically about three sets of style issues that have to do with business microwriting decisions: (1) how formal? (2) how passive? (3) how much jargon?

1. How formal?

Consider how formal you want to be, given your audience and the cultural context.

Too formal

- Sounds self-important, pompous, and blah; uses language you would never use in conversation; never shows wit, liveliness, or vigor
- Beats around the bush, never direct, and usually convoluted

Uses . . .

- Passive (as explained on the following page) to avoid responsibility ("A mistake was made") or just out of habit ("Your comments are appreciated" for "Thank you for your comments")
- "Weasel words" ("some may conclude that," "it may seem likely that")
- Unnecessarily long words and phrases ("pending determination of" for "until"; "utilization" for "use")
- Overlong sentences and paragraphs

Never uses . . .

- The imperative ("The line must be formed here" for "Form the line here").
- "I" (e.g., using your job title instead of using or "the undersigned" for "I")
- Contractions ("will be unable" for "won't be able")

Businesslike

- Sounds "business conversational"—which John Fielden describes as follows: "it is simple; it is personal; it is warm without being syrupy; it is forceful, like a firm handshake."

Uses . . .

- Short words and phrases, as you would in a business conversation
- Some contractions
- Personal pronouns when appropriate ("I," "you," or "we"), especially for positive or neutral messages.

Too informal

- Disorganized and rambling
- Inappropriate use of lowercase (e.g., at the beginnings of sentences or names)
- Slangy and overly casual
- Potentially insulting to unfamiliar older audiences, higher-ups, or clients by using (1) first names, (2) emoticons, and/or (3) TM and IM acronyms.

2. How passive?

A passive sentence always include or imply an action done by somebody or something—as opposed to an active sentence in which the active agent comes first ("his laptop was dropped" for "he dropped his laptop.")

Why you shouldn't use it: Research shows that the passive voice slows down your reader because (1) active sentences are shorter and clearer and (2) the reader must stop momentarily to figure out who is making the statement ("It is stated that" for "the Tax Code states").

When you should use it: Because of its disadvantages (which are especially important for busy business readers), use the passive only when needed (1) to de-emphasize the writer, (2) to avoid responsibility, or (3) for variety or other conscious reasons.

How you can convert it: To overcome its disadvantages, you can . . .

- *Turn the sentence around* ("The methods are explained in the appendices" to "The appendices explain the methods" for).
- *Change the verbs* (from "The website redesign is expected to achieve" to "The website redesign will probably achieve").
- *Rethink the sentence* (from "Improved relationships will be gained" to "This approach will yield maximum results").
- *Use the imperative* (from "Market share will be increased by" to "Increase market share"). The imperative provides two additional benefits, as well: it overcomes the problem of using too many *I's* and gives clear instructions or recommendations without sounding harsh.

3. How much jargon?

A third stylistic consideration is how much and what kind of jargon is appropriate in any given situation. Jargon is terminology associated with your field, and every profession has its own jargon. Here is an analysis of when using jargon is appropriate.

WHEN TO USE JARGON	
Yes if . . .	**No if . . .**
Written to readers in your field or with your background	Written to readers from different fields or backgrounds
Serves as a mutually understood shorthand	Creates misunderstanding, confusion, or exclusion
Saves time without losing reader comprehension	Wastes time by using ponderous expressions for simple ideas

The habit of using jargon with readers outside your field may be symptomatic of what former *Harvard Business Review* editor David Ewing calls "pathological professionalism." He asks, "Why do the perpetrators of these verbal monstrosities, knowing the material must be read and understood by innocent people, proceed with such sinister dedication? They rejoice in the difficulty of their trade. They find psychic rewards in producing esoteric and abstruse word combinations. They revel in the fact that only a small group, an elite counterculture, knows what in hell they are trying to say. Hence, the term *pathological professionalism*."

Chapters II, III, and IV (along with the Appendices) have covered ideas for managerial writing—summarized on the checklists on the following two pages. The next three chapters will turn to managerial speaking skills.

MACROWRITING CHECKLIST
Documents and Paragraphs
Chapter III

1. Document design for "high skim value"

1. Are your headings and subheadings effective?
   - Stand-alone sense?
   - Limited wording?
   - Parallel form?
2. Do you use white space effectively?
   - Shorter block of text?
   - White space for lists?
   - White space to show organization?
3. Do you use typography effectively?
   - For emphasis and consistency?
   - To show relative importance?

2. Signposts to show connection

1. Do the ideas in the document connect together?
   - Back and forth transitions?
   - Section previews?
2. Does your opening include a . . .
   - Common context?
   - Purpose for writing?
   - Overview of the structure?
3. Do you close effectively?
   - Feedback mechanism?
   - Action step?
   - Goodwill ending?

3. Effective paragraphs or sections

Does each paragraph have . . .

- Generalization followed by support?
- Signposts within the paragraph?

MICROWRITING CHECKLIST
Sentences and Words
Chapter IV

1. Brevity: Is your writing concise?
See pages 72–77.

Did you avoid . . .

- Wordiness?
- Overuse of linking verbs?
- Overuse of prepositions?
- Overlong sentences?

2. Style: Is your tone appropriate?
See pages 78–81.

1. How formal?
    - Too formal?
    - Businesslike?
    - Too informal?
2. How passive?
3. How much jargon?

3. Correctness
See Appendices, pages 160–172.

Have you used correct grammar and punctuation?

CHAPTER V OUTLINE

I. Tell/sell presentations
   1. Preparing what to say
   2. Preparing your notes

II. Questions and answers

III. Consult/join meetings
   1. Preparation before the meeting
   2. Participation during the meeting
   3. Decision making and follow-up

IV. Other speaking situations
   1. Manuscript speaking
   2. Impromptu speaking
   3. Webconferences
   4. Dealing with the media
   5. Team presentations

CHAPTER V

Speaking: Verbal Structure

In this chapter, we consider the verbal aspect of speaking—that is, what you say. In the following two chapters, we will look at the two other aspects of presentations: visual aids and nonverbal delivery skills.

Structuring what you say depends on the situation in which you are speaking. The chart below illustrates the three kinds of group speaking situations covered in this chapter: (1) tell/sell presentations, (2) questions and answers, and (3) consult/join meetings. This chapter also includes tips for other speaking situations: manuscript speaking, impromptu speaking, webconferences, dealing with the media, and team presentations.

SPEAKING: VERBAL STRUCTURE			
Section in this chapter	**I. Tell/Sell Presentations**	**II. Questions and Answers**	**III. Consult/Join Meetings**
Who speaks most	You	You in reaction to audience	Your audience
Possible purposes	To inform or to persuade	To answer questions	To discuss or to decide

I. TELL/SELL PRESENTATIONS

SPEAKING: VERBAL STRUCTURE			
Section in this chapter	**I. Tell/Sell Presentations**	**II. Questions and Answers**	**III. Consult/Join Meetings**
Who speaks most	You	You in reaction to audience	Your audience
Possible purposes	To inform or to persuade	To answer questions	To discuss or to decide

1. Preparing what to say

If you are speaking to inform or to persuade a group of people (regardless of whether in a stand-up presentation, a seated deck presentation, a videoconference, or a webcast), use these techniques to structure what you say. Since, unlike readers, your listeners can't glance back or skip ahead, you'll need to be repetitive and exceptionally clear by including (1) an opening, (2) a preview of the main points, (3) clearly demarcated main points, and (4) a closing.

Use an effective opening. Openings are important in all forms of communication, as we discussed with the Audience Memory Curve on page 19. When you make an oral presentation, however, your opening is even more crucial than it is when you write. Therefore, always use the first minute or so of your presentation for your opening, what many experts call a "grabber" or a "hook."

To decide what to say during your opening, think about the audience: Are they interested? Do they know how the topic relates to them? Do they know you well or not? Given your audience, choose from among the following techniques:

- *Tell them why you're speaking*—what they will learn in a tell presentation or what you hope they will do as a result of a sell presentation—so they can listen with these ideas in mind. (Refer to pages 20–21 regarding the direct structure.)

- *Grab their attention.* Why should they listen? Often, your audience will have other things on their minds or will not be especially interested in your topic, so you may need to open with a provocative question, a problem definition, a promise of what your presentation will deliver, a personal story that makes a business point, a vivid image, or a striking example or statistic.
- *Show them "what's in it for them" (WIIFT).* Why should they care? Why should they bother? Choose from among the best persuasion techniques on pages 15–17 with your particular audience in mind.
- *Build your credibility, if necessary.* If your audience doesn't know about you, introduce yourself and use any of the techniques discussed on pages 8–9 to enhance your credibility by establishing a "common ground."
- *Use humor with caution.* Humor can be an effective grabber; however, use it only if it fits your personality and style, if it is appropriate and inoffensive for every member of the audience, and if it relates to the topic or occasion. Never use humor that might make anyone feel left out, put down, or trivialized.

Next, give a preview. Without a doubt, the most important part of your presentation is a preview (also known as an agenda, an outline, or a table of contents) of what you will be covering. Always give an explicit preview at the beginning of your presentation.

Previews help your audience understand and remember what you say. Think again about the contrast between listeners and readers. Your readers can skim a document and read your headings and subheadings before they start reading. Your listeners, in contrast, have no idea what you will be covering unless you tell them.

Typical previews include a list of key points (such as reasons, examples, or recommendations), key questions, or a problem followed by a solution.

Examples of previews

> *Longer and more formal*: I will discuss sales in each of our four European regions: the Northern, Southern, Western, and Central.
>
> *Shorter and less formal:* Let's take a look at the sales figures in our four European regions.

State your main points clearly. Your main points need to be organized and easy to follow, much more so than in writing. Readers can look over, slow down, and reread when they wish; listeners, of course, cannot. Therefore, remember these three guidelines when you're speaking.

Limit your main points. Experiments in cognitive psychology show that people cannot easily comprehend more than five to seven main points, so do not exceed that number when you're speaking. That means grouping all of your points in any section or subsection into no more than seven major areas.

Use strong transitions. When you are speaking, you need longer, more explicit transitions between major sections and subsections than you do when you are writing. Listeners do not stay oriented as easily as readers do; they may not even remember what it is that you are listing unless you use these longer transitions.

Ineffective short transition

Second, . . .

Effective longer transitions

The second recommendation is . . .

Let's move on to the second recommendation.

Use backward look/forward look transitions. In addition to stronger, more explicit transitions, you also need to use more repetitive transitions when you're speaking, because listeners may not remember information they hear only once. Although you may feel as if you're being too repetitive, your listeners will appreciate detailed reminders that reinforce your structure. Therefore, between each major section and subsection, use a backward look/forward look transition. The backward look refers to recapping what you just covered, and the forward look provides a segue to the upcoming part of your talk.

Effective backward look/forward look transition

Now that we have looked at the three elements of the marketing plan **(backward look)**, let's turn to the financial implications of that plan **(forward look)**.

Keep their interest high. Since the Audience Memory Curve shows that your listeners' attention will decrease in the middle of your presentation, consider the following techniques to keep up their interest, involve them, add variety, and wake them up:

- *Include* stories, case illustrations, analogies, and examples—not just numbers.
- *Incorporate their names* (e.g., "Pat in accounting and Wahid in human resources" instead of "people from different departments").
- *Change your personal energy* (e.g., your tone, pauses, or nonverbal dynamism), as explained on pages 142–144.
- *Ask rhetorical questions* that relate to audience benefits (e.g., "So what does this mean for your business?").
- *Ask for a show of hands* (e.g., "How many of you think our current policy is effective?").
- *Tell them you'll be asking* for their input after the presentation.

Use an effective closing. The Audience Memory Curve also shows that your listeners are likely to remember your last words. Therefore, your closing should be more than a mere "thank you" or the all-too-common "dribble" closing like "I guess that's about it."

Instead, use a strong, obvious transitional phrase—such as "to summarize" or "in conclusion"—to introduce your closing remarks. Here are some options for effective closings:

- *Give a summary.* For a tell presentation, summarize your main points. Although this may feel repetitive to you, your audience will appreciate the wrap up.
- *End with the action steps.* For a sell presentation, "close the sale" by ending with the action steps, based on your communication objective. In addition, you might remind the audience "what's in it for them" if they take these action steps.
- *Refer to the opening.* A third kind of closing is to refer to the rhetorical question, promise, image, or story you used in your opening.
- *If you end with Q&A*, add a second closing, similar to your first one, so you get the last word.
- *If you run out of time*, do not try to rush through every point. Instead, concentrate on your main points only, especially your summary slide.

2. Preparing your notes

Another aspect of structuring a presentation has to do with the form your notes take. You certainly won't have the time to memorize every presentation you ever make; you will rarely have to read speeches verbatim; and you should never simply read your slides aloud word-for-word. Your audience deserves your eye contact and interaction, so instead of memorizing or reading, work from notes.

Notes will make you feel more confident because you can refer to them if necessary, without over relying on a word-for-word manuscript or subjecting yourself to the terror of speaking with no notes at all.

How to prepare your notes: The purpose of your notes is to jog your memory so you can spend most of your time looking at the audience, instead of reading. Therefore . . .

- *Do not write out complete sentences.* Instead, use very short phrases for each point or subpoint.
- *Consider tying your notes to your slides.* (1) Print out your slides four-per-page. Then add your notes and wording for backward look/forward look transitions (as discussed on page 88) around the slide copies. This method enhances your eye contact, because you will not be tempted to turn to the screen and read your slides.
- *Include about five minutes' worth of information* on each note card, so you are not constantly changing cards.
- *Use large enough lettering* (either handwritten or printed in a large font) so that you can read your note card at arm's length.
- *Leave enough white space* so that your cards are not cluttered or hard to read.
- *Add reminders to yourself* (optional), such as "Stand straight!" or "Show line chart here."

Cards versus paper: We suggest using 5×7 or 4×6 inch index cards—rather than 8½ × 11 inch paper. Think about the following advantages as you choose the method that feels more comfortable and looks less awkward for you.

- *Advantages of note cards:* Notes on index cards (1) are less noticeable to your audience than large pieces of paper; (2) are stiffer and easier to hold; (3) give you the ability to move around the room instead of being tied to a table or lectern; (4) allow you to add to, subtract from, or rearrange your material easily; and (5) may help you to use short phrases rather than complete sentences.
- *Advantage of paper:* Some speakers prefer using regular-sized paper for their notes, because they put their paper down on a desk, lectern, or table.

II. QUESTIONS AND ANSWERS

SPEAKING: VERBAL STRUCTURE			
Section in this chapter	**I. Tell/Sell Presentations**	**II. Questions and Answers**	**III. Consult/Join Meetings**
Who speaks most	You	You in reaction to audience	Your audience
Possible purposes	To inform or to persuade	To answer questions	To discuss or to decide

Most presentations involve interaction between the speaker and the audience in the form of questions and answers. Dealing effectively with questions and answers involves deciding when to take questions, how to take questions, what to say if you don't know the answer, and how to answer difficult questions.

When to take questions: Well before the presentation, think about when you will take questions. Then be sure to inform your audience at the beginning of the presentation. Say, for example, "Please feel free to ask questions as they come up" or "Please hold all your questions until the end of the presentation" or "Feel free to interrupt with questions of understanding or clarification, but since we only have an hour together, please hold questions of debate or discussion until the end."

Usually, audience and cultural expectations are fairly clear: the current trend in most business presentations in the United States is to include questions during the presentation; sometimes, however, the norm is for a question-and-answer period at the end of the presentation. If the choice is up to you, think about the following advantages and disadvantages.

- *Holding questions until the end*: If you take questions after the presentation, you will maintain control over the schedule and the flow of information. However, you risk (1) losing your audience's attention, and perhaps even comprehension, if they cannot interrupt with their questions and (2) placing yourself in an awkward position if important audience members interrupt with questions after you've asked them not to. Because audiences tend to remember more material from the beginning and the end of a presentation, however, having "Q&A" last places undue emphasis on the question period. To alleviate this problem, leave your summary slide displayed during the questions and save time for a two- to three-minute summary after the questions.
- *Taking questions throughout:* If you take questions during the presentation, the questions will be more meaningful to the questioner, the feedback will be more immediate, and your audience may listen more actively. However, questions during the presentation can upset your schedule and waste time. To alleviate these problems, (1) budget 20% extra time for questions and (2) control digressions using the skills described on the following pages.

How to take questions: Once you've established when to take questions, prepare yourself for how you will take them.

- *Prepare in advance:* Prepare yourself by anticipating possible questions. Try to guess what the questions will be. Bring along extra information, perhaps even extra slides, to answer such questions if they come up. Another way to anticipate questions is to ask a colleague to play devil's advocate during your rehearsal.

  Try to expect and value questions. Instead of going in with a defensive attitude, think of it as a compliment if your listeners are interested enough to ask for clarification, amplification, or justification.

  Frequently asked questions include those of (1) *value* ("Are you sure we really need this?" or "What will happen if we don't do this?"), (2) *cost* ("Can we do it for less?"), (3) *action* ("How can we do it?" or "Will this action cause new problems?"), and (4) *details* ("What is your source?" or "Is that number correct?").

- *Show your understanding:* When someone asks a question, listen carefully to be sure you understand it before you answer. Paraphrase or summarize complicated questions to make sure you're on the right track. Use effective listening skills: maintain eye contact, nod, and do not interrupt.

- *Stick to your objective and your organization:* Answer the question, but always stay on message. Even if you know a lot of information for your answer, limit yourself to whatever advances your objective. Don't go off on rambling tangents. If necessary, divert the question back to your main ideas. If someone asks a question you had planned to cover later in your talk, try to answer it in a nutshell and then make it clear that you will cover it in more detail later.
- *Keep everyone involved:* Keep the entire audience involved by calling on people from various locations in the audience and by avoiding a one-to-one conversation with a single audience member. When you answer, maintain eye contact with the entire audience, not just with the person who asked the question. Also, avoid ending your answer by looking right at the questioner; he or she may feel invited to ask another question.

What to say if you don't know the answer: Sometimes, you absolutely don't know the answer; other times you just need time to gather your thoughts.

- *If you don't know:* If you don't know the answer, say, "I don't know." Even better, suggest where the person might find the answer. Better still, offer to get the answer yourself. For example, "Off the top of my head, I don't know the market share in that country, but I'll look it up and email it to you by tomorrow morning." Never hazard a guess unless you make it extremely clear that it is only a guess.
- *If you need some time to think:* If you are momentarily stymied by a question, here are some techniques to buy yourself some thinking time. (1) *Repeat*: "You're wondering how to deal with this situation." (2) *Turn the question around*: "How would *you* deal with this situation?" (3) *Turn the question outward*: "How would the rest of you deal with this situation?" (4) *Reflect*: "Good question. Let's think about that for a moment." (5) *Write*: If you are using a suitable visual aid, write down the main point of the question as you think.

How to answer challenging questions: Some questions are especially challenging because they are confusing, controlling, or hostile.

- *Confusing questions:* Confusing questions may be long, rambling, multifaceted, or overly broad. In these cases, paraphrase the question before you answer, refocusing to make it appropriate for your communication objective. If the questioner repeats the inappropriately long version of the question, something like "I wish we had more time so we could discuss that" or "Let's explore that in more detail after the presentation is over."
- *Controlling questions:* Some questions are not really questions; they are statements. In the case of these mini-lectures, do not feel obliged to answer or to ask "So what exactly is your question?" Instead, thank them for their comments, perhaps even paraphrasing their ideas, and then proceed with your presentation.

  Other controlling questions are those questions that the audience member clearly wants to answer him- or herself or that focus on his or her interests only. In these cases, you need to decide whether you want to (1) regain control yourself by refocusing on your communication objective or (2) change your focus midstream by turning the question back to them ("What do you think we ought to do?"). For example, if you were explaining a new procedure to a large group of employees, you would probably opt to regain control; if you were talking to a small group of important clients, you would probably choose to change focus to meet their needs.
- *Hostile questions*: People may be hostile because of lack of information; in these cases, you can influence them through facts and logic. Many times, however, they may be hostile because they feel passionate, threatened, defensive, isolated, or resentful of change. Faced with a hostile question, take a deep breath, identify the hostility ("I understand you feel upset about this"), and answer the question nonemotionally and nonpersonally. Sometimes, you may be able to find a common ground ("We're both trying to do what we feel is in the customer's best interest"). Sometimes, however, you have no choice but to agree to disagree, paraphrasing both points of view clearly.

III. CONSULT/JOIN MEETINGS

SPEAKING: VERBAL STRUCTURE			
Section in this chapter	**I. Tell/Sell Presentations**	**II. Questions and Answers**	**III. Consult/Join Meetings**
Who speaks most	You	You in reaction to audience	Your audience
Possible purposes	To inform or to persuade	To answer questions	To discuss or to decide

Unlike either a tell/sell presentation (in which you do most of the speaking) or a Q&A session (in which you have limited audience interaction), in a consult/join meeting, you are discussing or deciding as a group (with extensive participant interaction). Although this section focuses on face-to-face meetings, most of the techniques apply equally to webmeetings. (For an analysis of webmeetings as a channel, see page 28. For techniques to handle the technical side of these internet-based meetings, see page 100.)

Many businesspeople erroneously assume that running a meeting is easy, simple, and straightforward. Actually, meeting facilitation involves a complex and difficult set of tasks.

According to negotiation expert Lindsay Rahmun, meetings are difficult because of a set of inherent contradictions, which she dubs "the participant's dilemma." (1) We expect people to be thoughtful and innovative, yet simultaneously fast and efficient; (2) We are annoyed when people don't participate, yet annoyed when they talk too much; (3) We expect people to offer their best ideas, yet not get defensive when those ideas are modified or rejected; (4) We want to hold high standards of quality and resist "groupthink," yet at the same time, we call people stubborn and inflexible if they don't move with the group; (5) We want to work with a small group for efficiency, yet with a large group for inclusiveness.

Following are some guidelines for dealing with three complex sets of issues: preparation before the meeting, participation during the meeting, and decision making and follow-up after the meeting. For much more information about meeting management, see *Guide to Meetings* (cited on page 176).

I. Preparation before the meeting

Before the meeting, think carefully about the meeting objective, agenda, and roles. See page 6 to analyze when to call a meeting instead of choosing another channel of communication.

Set the objective. Perhaps the single most prevalent complaint about meetings is that they are called unnecessarily. Meetings should be reserved for situations in which you need group discussion, not for routine announcements or for presenting your own finalized ideas.

Set the agenda. Because the whole purpose of a meeting is to elicit information from other people, prepare your agenda carefully and in advance, so that participants can think of ideas ahead of time. Your agenda should (1) state the meeting objective and (2) let participants know exactly how they should prepare in advance and what they will be expected to contribute.

Delegate roles. Decide what role(s) you are going to perform yourself—and which you will delegate to someone else. (1) *Facilitator:* You might ask someone else to facilitate the meeting if you wish to be an active participant yourself. (2) *Timer:* Consider asking a different person to time the meeting because it's difficult to concentrate on the discussion and keep your mind on the time all at once. (3) *Minutes writer:* You may also want to appoint someone else to write up minutes after the meeting. (4) *Scribe:* Finally, instead of choosing to record participant comments during the meeting yourself, consider asking someone else to serve as scribe. This increasingly popular technique makes you more effective because you don't have to write and talk simultaneously; improves legibility because the scribe has more time to write; and increases meeting energy and saves meeting time because you can go on to discuss the next point while the scribe is still recording the previous point.

2. Participation during the meeting

Here are some techniques to increase participation . . .

Opening the meeting: At the beginning of the meeting, plan to . . .

- *Start on time.*
- *Explain the agenda.*
- *Get people to agree on ground rules.* Examples of ground rules include the following: "We will start and stop on time." "We will not interrupt." "We will treat all information as confidential."
- *Involve people early.* The earlier you can get participants involved in some way, the more likely they are to participate.

During the meeting: Throughout the meeting . . .

- *Ask open-ended questions.* Ask questions that cannot be answered "yes" or "no," such as "How should we attack this problem?" or "What are your reactions to this proposal?"
- *Paraphrase their responses.* Restate their ideas concisely, such as "So what you're suggesting is . . . "
- *Record their responses.* Either you or your scribe should record participants' ideas on a board or chart in full public view.
- *Use "minimal encouragers."* Use minimal encouragers—such as "I see," "OK," or "uh huh"—to keep the discussion going.
- *Handle disagreement carefully.* Do not show your disagreement too soon (e.g., "That won't work because" or "I disagree because"). State disagreements carefully; disagree with ideas, not with people personally.
- *Don't talk too much.* You have called the meeting for their input, so don't dominate it by talking too much yourself.

3. Decision making and follow-up

Don't waste the valuable ideas you gained from the meeting participants; use the following techniques to make a decision and to follow up.

Decision making: For those items on your agenda that require a decision, make it clear to the participants in advance which decision-making method you plan to use.

- *By one person or majority vote:* These two methods are quite fast and are effective when the decision is not particularly important or when you face severe time constraints. Their disadvantage, however, is that some people may feel left out, ignored, or defeated—and these people may later sabotage the implementation.
- *By consensus:* Consensus means reaching a compromise that may not be everybody's first choice, but is an option everyone can live with. Consensus involves hearing all points of view and incorporating these viewpoints into the solution, so it is time consuming and requires group commitment to the process. Unlike majority rule, consensus is reached by discussion, not by a vote. For example, the facilitator might ask, "Do you all feel comfortable with this solution?" or "Seems to me we've reached consensus around this idea. Am I right?" Consensus does not mean unanimity; no participant has veto power.

Follow-up: At the close of the meeting, take the time to figure out how you are going to follow up with a permanent record and an action plan.

- *Permanent record:* Most meetings should be documented with a permanent record of some kind, usually called the "minutes," to record what occurred and to communicate those results. Effective minutes include the issues discussed, alternatives considered, decisions reached, and action plan.
- *Action plan:* The group should agree on an action plan, to include (1) actions to be taken, (2) person responsible for each action, and (3) a time frame for each action.

IV. OTHER SPEAKING SITUATIONS

In addition to the three standard speaking situations already covered in this chapter, you may find yourself in other kinds of situations. This section offers some additional techniques for dealing with (1) manuscript speaking, (2) impromptu speaking, (3) webconferences, (4) media interaction, and (5) team presentations.

1. Manuscript speaking: Occasionally you may find yourself called on to speak word-for-word from a manuscript. If so, use the "spoken style": (1) avoiding phrases that no one would actually say in conversation; (2) using a large font and short sentences; (3) leaving the bottom third of the page blank so that your head will not drop too low as you read; (4) finishing a sentence or paragraph before any page break; (5) leaving the pages unstapled, so you can slide the completed page to the side; and (6) underlining key words for vocal emphasis.

2. Impromptu speaking: Impromptu speaking means talking on the spur of the moment, without advance preparation. For example, your boss may suddenly ask you to "bring us up to date on a certain service." Usually, of course, you will not be asked to make impromptu remarks unless you have some knowledge in the area.

Here are some suggestions to help you in impromptu speaking situations: (1) *Anticipate.* Try to avoid truly impromptu situations. Guess at the probability of your being called on during discussions, meetings, or interviews. Guess at the topics you might be asked to discuss. (2) *Relate to experience.* You will speak more easily and confidently if you try to relate the topic to your specific experiences and to the topics you know best. (3) *Keep your remarks short.* Say what you have to say and then stop. Do not ramble on, feeling that you must deliver a lengthy lecture. (4) *Start with a preview*, if possible. You will sound more intelligent and make your remarks easier to follow.

3. Webconferences: Webmeetings, webinars, and webcasts are the internet equivalents of consult/join meetings and tell/sell presentations. Their venue can range from a large room to a boardroom to desktop computers.

Unlike face-to-face meetings and presentations, however, these channels offer many advantages: reaching a geographically-dispersed audience in multiple locations simultaneously; saving on travel time and money; allowing for collaboration by using document sharing; and reaching extremely large audiences. (See pages 26–28 for a more detailed analysis of these channels of communication.)

You can gain many of the same advantages, however, by using telephone conference calls. So, choose conference calls unless you really need to see the audience. Conference calls will save money, add scheduling flexibility, and decrease your chances for technical glitches.

When using the web-based channels, keep in mind the following guidelines.

Plan the conference.

- Set the objective and agenda; select and invite participants; distribute materials in advance; and prepare graphics and visual aids. (See pages 95–98 for meeting details.)
- Assign a leader for each site. Get a phone number to call if the conference suddenly disconnects.
- Work around multiple time zones and arrange for translators or a taped archival copy, if appropriate.
- Rehearse in advance with the equipment. If possible, critique yourself on tape.
- Send your slides or documents electronically to other sites ahead of time.

Plan with the technician.

- Before the day of the conference, have your technician do a "tech check," connecting to the other site(s) to make sure everything connects and is compatible. As part of that tech check: (1) think about how both the speaker(s) and the slides will be shown; (2) discuss camera angles (try to arrange for close-ups of the person talking instead of a long shot of everyone in the room); and (3) check the sound for volume and lack of echoes.

- Make sure you know how to deal with the slide projector or document camera, mute the sound, and change camera angles during the conference.
- Arrange to have a technician (1) come in right before the conference to recheck the equipment and (2) be on call during the conference—either in the room or nearby—to deal with technical glitches. Make sure you have the telephone numbers of the technicians at the other sites as well.

Enhance your body language.

- Be yourself; look confident; don't be afraid to smile; talk to the participants as if they were sitting across from you.
- Love the camera. Emotion is captivating, so show some. Show more than you normally might show in a face-to-face meeting.
- Move your head. Your head and shoulders may be most of what your audience will see. Therefore, do what TV announcers do—nodding, shaking their heads, raising their eyebrows, and so on.
- Avoid any quick movements; use slow, restrained hand gestures; avoid any quirky mannerisms, such as fiddling with your glasses or tapping your pen.
- Assume you're always "on stage": avoid side conversations; sit naturally, neither stone-still nor squirming.

Enhance your voice.

- *Speak naturally and conversationally*, with pauses and inflection. However, speak a bit more slowly, deliberately, and loudly than usual, without shouting.
- *Avoid unwanted sounds*, such as, coughing into microphone, tapping your fingers or pencil near microphone, breathing heavily, rattling papers, or jingling coins.
- *Remember to pause* so that others may speak.
- *Keep your remarks brief* and conversational.

For more on running meetings in general, see pages 95–98 and *Guide to Meetings,* cited in the bibliography on page 176.

4. Dealing with the media: Here are some techniques to use for media interviews.

Preparing in advance

- *Cultivate and maintain media relationships.* (1) Get to know the reporters who cover your industry and company. (2) Find out about the reporters who are interviewing you. Look at their previous stories or watch previous shows—watching for their biases; favorite themes; interview formats; and use of charts, graphs, or bullet points. Prepare information the way they prefer to receive it.
- *Analyze two audiences.* Analyze both the reporter and the readers or viewers.
- *Think of questions in advance.* If possible, find out in advance from the reporters what topics or questions they intend to ask. In addition, brainstorm possible questions: If you were the reporter, what would you ask? What would the audience be interested in? Ask colleagues and potential audience members to brainstorm questions.
- *Plan your responses in advance.* Think about what you want to communicate and what main messages you want to get across. Structure these messages into short, crisp statements, sometimes known as "sound bites."

Responding during the interview

- *Listen carefully.* Think before responding. Answer only the question you were asked.
- *Use "bridging"* to move from the reporters' questions to your main-message sound bites.
- *Bring your points to life* by using short anecdotes, analogies, and simple statistics.

Being on camera

- *Prepare for mechanical distractions.* Rehearse on set to learn cues and see the equipment.
- *Decide where to focus.* If you are recording by yourself, you will probably look directly at the camera; if you are appearing on a talk show, you will probably look at the host.
- *Dress appropriately.* (1) Wear light-colored clothing (not white) and solid colors, such as blue, gray, or pastels. (2) Avoid plaids, patterns, prints, black, red, and the color of the backdrop. (3) Keep jewelry subtle and simple.

For more information on dealing with the media, see the *Guide to Media Relations* cited in the bibliography on page 176.

5. Team presentations: Make sure your team presentations are organized, unified, and coherent—not simply an unrelated series of individual presentations.

Organize as a whole. The major problem with team presentations occurs when each presenter prepares a separate part, and the parts never coalesce into a coherent whole. To avoid this problem, compose the agenda before you even think about who will say what. In other words, structure the agenda by the appropriate number of content topic sections, not by the number of members you happen to have in your team. After the agenda is completed, decide the speaking order, remembering that one speaker may cover two content sections, or one content section may be covered by multiple speakers.

Provide content transitions between speakers. To begin, one team member should provide the opening and preview for the presentation as a whole, introducing the team members and the topics they will cover. Then, after each speaker finishes, he or she should provide a backward look/forward look transition (as explained on page 88), such as "Now that I have explained our proposal (**backward look**), Tyrone will explain the financial implications of that proposal (**forward look**)."

Use visual aids consistently. Your visuals should look team designed, not individually designed. (1) *Use the same template* or overall design throughout (e.g., the same colors, fonts, and sizes, as covered on pages 111–117). (2) *Interact with your visuals consistently* (e.g., how you use the remote or animation, as explained on pages 133–136.)

Rehearse and deliver as a group. In your first run-through—or what speaking expert Antony Jay calls the "stagger-through"—practice what you will say, the exact wording of your transitions, and rough drafts of your visuals. In a second run-through, work to perfect your delivery and flow.

Choreograph your logistics. Remember that you are all "on stage" from the moment you walk into the room. Therefore, (1) *Plan exactly* how you will start, seat the nonspeakers, "hand off" to one another, finish, and take questions (Who will moderate and direct questions? How will you sit?), and (2) *Maintain professional nonverbal behavior* while others speak: look attentive and avoid side conversations.

CHAPTER VI OUTLINE

I. Designing the presentation as a whole
   1. Translate your structure into draft slides.
   2. Tie your slides together with connectors.
   3. Differentiate between slides and decks.

II. Designing your Slide Master
   1. Selecting colors
   2. Choosing a readable font
   3. Using animation to "build" your ideas

III. Designing each individual slide
   1. Using message titles
   2. Designing graphical charts to show "how much"
   3. Designing concept diagrams to show "how"
   4. Designing text slides to show "why" and "how"
   5. Using other visual images
   6. Editing each slide

IV. Practicing with visual aids
   1. General preparation techniques
   2. Techniques for specific equipment

CHAPTER VI

Speaking: Visual Aids

No matter how well you have prepared what you are going to say (Chapter V) or how skilled you may be in your nonverbal speaking delivery (Chapter VII), your audience still has the capacity to daydream: they can think faster than you can speak. To keep them concentrating on your ideas, provide visual aids that back up what you're saying. Visual aids . . .

- *Add* interest, variety, and impact
- *Increase audience comprehension* and retention
- *Remain in the memory* longer than just words
- *Reach 40% of your audience* who are likely to be visual, rather than auditory, learners

Here are some techniques to use for (1) designing the visual presentation as a whole, (2) designing each individual slide, (3) choosing the equipment, and (4) using visuals effectively.

VISUAL AIDS			
I. Designing the presentation as a whole	II. Designing your Slide Master	III. Designing each individual slide	IV. Practicing with visual aids

I. DESIGNING THE PRESENTATION AS A WHOLE

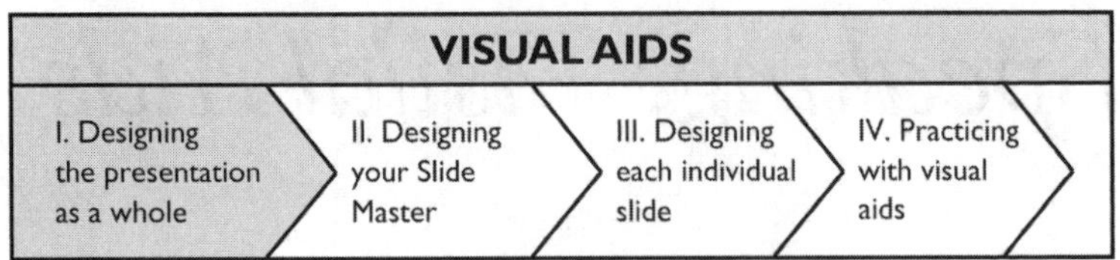

This section describes a three-step process for designing your visuals for the presentation. Think through these macro issues first, before you start composing individual slides, as described in Part II, the second main section of this chapter.

1. Translate your structure into draft slides.

The first step is to translate your structure (as discussed on pages 86–89) into draft slides.

Closing and agenda slides: Compose your closing and agenda slides first—and in tandem—to ensure that you emphasize your main take-aways at both the beginning and the end of your presentation. (See the Audience Memory Curve on page 19.) Make sure that both slides . . .

- *Make stand-alone sense* (as explained on pages 54–55) and illustrated on the example on the facing page.
- *Use the presentation title* (not just "Summary," "Thank you," "Any questions?" or "Agenda").
- *Are highly visible* by (1) displaying the agenda slide extra-slowly, using animation to build each point and (2) keeping the closing slide visible during Q&A and at the end of your presentation.

Ineffective closing/agenda slide

Agenda
• Overview
• Product
• Market Analysis
• Competition
• Operations
• Summary
Title lacks "stand-alone sense"
Unnecessary to state on agenda slide
Not conceptually parallel
Bullets lack "stand-alone sense"

Effective closing/agenda slide

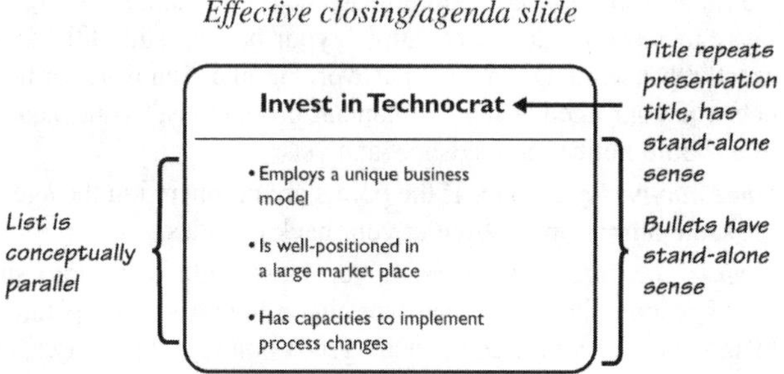

Backup slides: Backup slides explain, or "back up," each point on the agenda. Therefore . . .

- Prepare one or more backup slides to explain each agenda item.
- Make sure all of your backup slides follow from, and relate back to, the agenda—as explained on the next two pages.

Opening slide (optional): While you are grabbing your audience's interest (pages 86–87), you may choose to display any one of the following:

- *Blank screen* to keep the spotlight on you and your words, rather than on a competing visual.
- *Title slide*, visually reinforcing the subject of the presentation.
- *Grabber slide*—such as a striking photograph, quotation, or statistic—to help arouse your audience's interest.

2. Tie your slides together with connectors.

Throughout the presentation, you need to keep your audience reminded of where you are on your agenda, so they can keep anchored to the main points at all times. Here are three options to provide connectors between your agenda and each backup slide:

Consistency: One easy but powerful connector is to observe scrupulous consistency.

- *Same phrasing:* If you have one or two backup slides for each agenda point, make sure that the slide heading in each backup slide uses exactly the same wording you used in the agenda. For example, if your agenda says "Increase product innovation," your backup slide title should use exactly that wording—not similar wording like "Innovate for new products"; if your agenda says "Financial projections," your backup slide title should not be "Spreadsheet analysis."
- *Same numbering system:* If the points are numbered in the agenda, use the same numbering system in your backup slides.
- *Similar phrasing in trackers*: If you have multiple backup slides for each agenda point, use similar wording in the trackers (explained on the facing page) as you used in each agenda point. In these cases, the message title of each slide should relate to the main idea of the slide itself, not that of the agenda slide.

Repeated agenda: Another effective connector to remind your audience what you have already covered and what you will cover next is to display your agenda slide repeatedly throughout the presentation, each time you switch to the next main section in your agenda. When you repeat your agenda, use a method to emphasize the upcoming section, such as . . .

- *Highlight the text* of the upcoming section in a different color.
- *Dim the text* of the sections you are not covering next.
- *Put a box* around the text of the upcoming section.
- *Insert an arrow* pointing to the upcoming section.

Examples of repeated agendas

Trackers: If your presentation is especially long or complex, consider using "trackers" on each backup slide to connect your slides together clearly. Trackers serve the same purpose as the "running header" at the top of the pages of this and other books—that is, reminding the audience what section you are currently discussing.

- *What they are:* Trackers are a shortened version of each main point on the agenda, with each point reduced to one or two words.
- *Where they appear:* As shown in the following examples, trackers usually appear across the bottom of the slide, the lower right-hand corner, or the upper left-hand corner—where they are visible, but not emphatic (e.g., in a smaller font and muted color). Do not use a tracker on the title, agenda, or summary slides.

Heading heading heading

- Bullet text bullet text
- Bullet text bullet text
- Bullet text bullet text

Tracker 1 • Tracker 2 • Tracker 3

Heading heading heading

- Bullet text bullet text
- Bullet text bullet text
- Bullet text bullet text

Tracker

Tracker

Heading heading heading

- Bullet text bullet text
- Bullet text bullet text
- Bullet text bullet text

- *What they look like:* Here are some guidelines for designing your trackers. (1) *Size:* Trackers need to be visible, but avoid calling too much attention to themselves. Therefore, use the smallest size your audience can read. (2) *For text agendas:* Trackers should be a shortened version of each main point. In such cases, reduce the wording of each main point to one or two words. (3) *For diagram agendas* (such as chevrons or a pyramid): Trackers may be a mini-version of the diagram. However, never use a diagram for a tracker unless you used the same diagram in the agenda.
- *What they include*: Trackers can include either (1) *the current section* that you are discussing at the moment or (2) *all of the main sections*, with the current point visually highlighted (e.g., in boldface or a different shade).
- *What they do not include:* (1) Do not insert trackers on your title, agenda, or summary slides. (2) Do not include the agenda or summary on your list of trackers: trackers list your main sections only.

3. Differentiate between slides and decks.

Your decision to make a slide presentation (with projected slides) or a deck presentation (with a paper deck) will have an enormous impact on the overall design of your visual aids. The chart below summarizes the differences between the two:

COMPARING SLIDES AND DECKS		
	SLIDES usually . . .	**DECKS** usually . . .
Focus on ... **Supported by...**	The speaker The projected slides	The printed deck The speaker
Discussion	Usually less	Usually more
Speaker	Standing	Usually seated
Font	Visible from back of the room; large for titles, medium-sized for text	Visible when viewed on a table; medium-sized for titles, smaller for text
Detail	Limited detail	More detail than slides, but much less than Word documents
Preview visual	Preview/agenda slide	Table of Contents page
Cueing the audience	By using animation to build content and accent color to refer to specific elements	By page number and by referring to elements on charts, diagrams, and lists
Background color	Dark for formal; light for less formal	Usually white; sometimes colored
Charts and diagrams	Must be simplified; can use "build"	Can be more complex; can't use "build"
Last-minute changes possible	Yes	No
"Deck" is called	"Slideshow deck"	"Discussion deck"

II. DESIGNING YOUR SLIDE MASTER

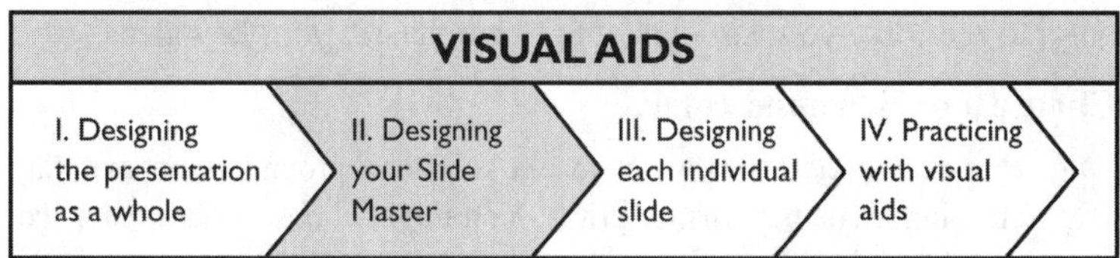

Follow the composition process explained on pages 36–44 to compose your slides. In other words, do not even open PowerPoint (or other such program) until you have organized and drafted your slides on paper. Only after you have this draft (or "storyboard") is it time to translate that draft into PowerPoint. The trick is to take charge of your PowerPoint, instead of letting its defaults take charge of you.

Design your own Slide Master. Your first task is to design your own Slide Master—a master template that will make your colors and fonts automatic and consistent throughout. Why should you design a Slide Master when the software has more than 40 design templates available? The reason is that virtually all of the PowerPoint templates are inappropriate for business presentations: they are full of visual distractions (such as graphics, patterns, shimmers, textures, or fades) that make the slides hard to read. Or in the words of PowerPoint critic Edward Tufte, "No matter how beautiful your PP readymade template is, it would be better if there were less of it."

Or at least choose a plain one. If you must use one of PowerPoint's built-in design templates, consider one of the following templates that are less distracting than others: Blends, Edge, Network, and Pixel. On the other hand, some of the least business-appropriate design templates include Crayons, Curtain Call, Fireworks, Maple, Mountain Top, and Proposal.

Instead of ready-made templates, then, design your own Slide Master, choosing (1) colors, (2) font, and (3) animation.

1. Selecting colors

Use color consistently throughout the presentation for two reasons only: to reinforce your structure and to emphasize your key ideas.

Choose a background color.

- *Projected slides:* Always choose a solid background color, avoiding any shimmers, patterns, or prints. You might choose a dark color like dark blue, dark green, or black. Another choice would be to use a different darker color for the title placeholder area, or insert a plain-colored line to separate the title from the text. Or, for a less formal look, you might select a light color such as cream, beige, or white.
- *Decks:* White or light colors are the best background choices for decks.

Choose title and text colors.

- *Projected slides:* Choose a color that contrasts sharply with your background color, such as yellow or white on a dark background or black or dark blue on a light background.
- *Decks*: Usually use black for title and text colors in a deck, although other bold or dark colors will also work for a color deck.

Choose an accent color. Your background and text colors will set up a pattern that will keep your viewers better attuned to your structure, because they sense patterns of color quickly and subconsciously. Whenever you use a color that deviates from this consistent pattern, your viewers' eyes will be drawn immediately to that accent color, also known as "spot color" or "spotlight color." So, select a bright, contrasting accent color and . . .

- *Use your accent color sparingly.* Use accent color carefully—only when you want to lead your audience's eyes to a particular place for emphasis. Think of your accent color as a spotlight that draws your audience's attention to a certain specific place on your slide. For example, you might want to spotlight a certain column, a certain bar, or a certain piece on a pie chart. Or you could spotlight an arrow to point at a certain place on a diagram.
- *Do not use accent color for unimportant elements.* Don't waste the power of your accent color by using it for unimportant items—such as the bullet character itself, a line, a border, or those "fruit salad" PowerPoint defaults that make each bar, column, etc. a different color. Instead, reserve the accent color only for that which is the most important on the slide.

- *Link accent color to message titles.* You can often use your accent color to emphasize your main point. The examples below show accent color used to reinforce each of the two message titles by highlighting "the final stage" and the "East."

Examples: accent color linked to message titles

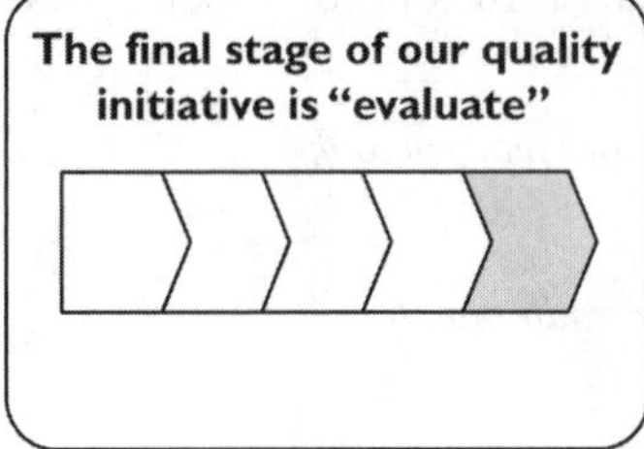

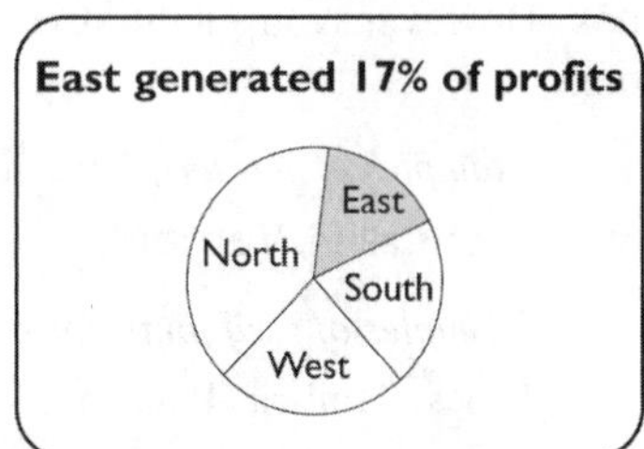

- *Use accent color and visual elements as a pointer* if you want to highlight a specific point on your slide.

Examples: accent color used as a "pointer"

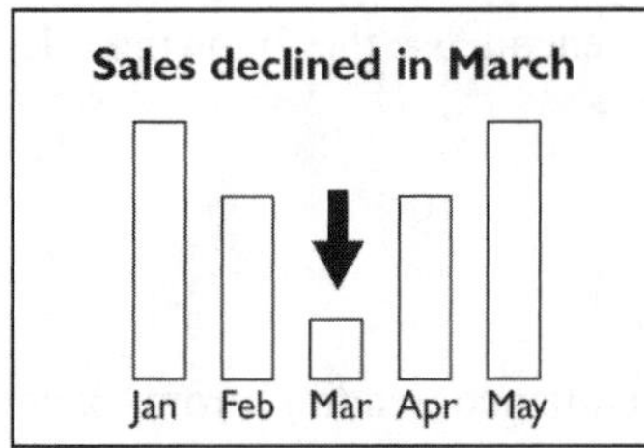

Evaluate your quality efforts

- Complete peer reviews.
- Fill out quality survey.
- Submit by May 24

Avoid the "fruit salad effect." By controlling your color choices (and not allowing PowerPoint's defaults to take over), you can avoid what design expert Jan White has dubbed the "fruit salad effect," such as a pie chart with every single wedge a different color. This profusely colorful combination may be attractive in a fruit salad, but it is distracting and confusing on a slide.

Always check your colors on the big screen. Always check your colors on the large screen, not just on your computer monitor. What you see on the screen will never be the same as what you see on your monitor. All the work you put into designing the consistent look on your Slide Master will be wasted if you forget this important step.

2. Choosing a readable font.

In addition to your template colors, think about your template typography—including font type, size, case, and style.

Presenters usually choose a sans serif font (that is, a font without extensions or "feet" on the end of letter) for a more contemporary look. However, you might also choose a serif font for a more classic look.

Examples of san serif fonts, for a more modern look

Arial, Calibri, Verdana

Examples of serif fonts, for a more traditional look

Times, Cambria, Palatino

Make sure your letters are large enough. Choose large enough letter sizes for your entire audience to read your slides easily.

For on-screen presentations, check the font size by standing eight feet away from your monitor, or better yet, by sitting at the back of the room where you will be presenting. In general, use the following rules of thumb:

- *Headings:* 28–32 point
- *Text:* 18–24 point
- *Labels:* 14 point

For deck presentations, with the audience reading from paper instead of looking at a screen, use larger font sizes than you would in other printed documents—because (1) your audience is listening and talking at the same time, not just reading and (2) the document is on a table, not held up closer to their eyes. Therefore, use approximately . . .

- *Headings:* 16 point
- *Text:* 14 point
- *Labels:* 12 point

For locking in your choices, be sure to override an annoying feature of PowerPoint that will downsize the size of your text automatically to cram it all into the space available. For detailed instructions on how to do this (as well as all of the other PowerPoint issues in this chapter), refer to *Guide to PowerPoint,* cited on page 176.

Use sentence case for text. From among the following three kinds of "case," choose sentence case (defined below) for extended text.

AS YOU CAN SEE FROM READING THESE LINES, EXTENDED USE OF UPPERCASE, USING ALL CAPITAL LETTERS, SLOWS DOWN THE READER AND IMPAIRS READABILITY; THEREFORE, USE UPPERCASE SPARINGLY.

Avoid Using Title Case With All Initial Caps Like This For Extended Text Because Title Case Causes Pointless Bumps In The Lines That Slow Down The Reader.

Instead, use sentence case like this, because it shows the shape of each word and is therefore easier to process.

Use font styles sparingly. Do not overuse font styles (such as bold and italics). Instead . . .

- Use font styles sparingly, for emphasis only.
- Never use such styles for extended text.
- Stick to the basics of bold and italics; other styles may impair readability.

Examples of font styles

You might choose bold for titles.

You might choose italics for subtitles only, but never for extended text like these sentences. Because italicized letters are slanted and lighter than regular type, they are harder to read for extended text like this.

Choose your design cascade. All of your font choices combined will result in a design cascade (as explained in more detail on pages 24–25). For example, a centered title looks more emphatic than a title; a boldface subhead looks more emphatic than an italicized one.

3. Using animation to "build" your ideas.

Animation is the PowerPoint tool that allows you "build"—that is, systematically disclose—one bullet point or one chart component at a time.

Use animation to focus audience attention. Use animation (perhaps in conjunction with your accent color) to keep your audience focused on the point you are currently making. If you don't use animation, and simply display the entire slide at once, the audience may read ahead or become confused figuring out which point you are discussing. Always think about the best ways to use this function.

Choose "Appear" as your animation effect. PowerPoint offers a variety of animation effects and sounds—such as flying, dissolving, dropping down, swiveling, wiping, and even checkerboarding. Such excessive animation, with text or graphics flying in from every side and spinning around, distracts your audience. Therefore, in general, choose the "Appear" effect, in which your next point simply appears all at once.

Build important bullet text. Your listeners will always read ahead of what you are discussing. Therefore, use builds on any slide in which you want to emphasize or discuss slowly—such as your agenda slide or bullet lists. You don't need to animate every single bullet on every single slide. Instead, make a conscious choice about what really needs to be animated.

Build complex charts. If you display a complex chart all at once, your audience will be trying to figure out what it is and how it works instead of listening to you. Therefore, build complicated charts gradually, explaining each new element as you add it.

Use animation as your pointer. Always use PowerPoint as your "pointer": avoid pointing vaguely in the direction of the screen or, even worse, using the dreaded laser pointer—which is not only far too small for your audience to see easily, but usually jiggles and shakes around on the screen. Therefore, as you design your Slide Master . . .

- *Think about how you will use PowerPoint as a pointer.* For example, you can insert arrows, lines, circles, boxes, symbols, or words to direct your audience's eyes exactly where you want them to look.
- *Use it in conjunction with your accent color* to further spotlight the image or words you have chosen.

For much more information about PowerPoint, including explicit "point-and-click" directions, see *Guide to PowerPoint*, cited on page 176.

III. DESIGNING EACH INDIVIDUAL SLIDE

VISUAL AIDS

I. Designing the presentation as a whole	II. Designing your Slide Master	III. Designing each individual slide	IV. Practicing with visual aids

Once you have planned your presentation as a whole, as discussed in the previous section, then design each individual slide. This section covers the following design techniques to do so: (1) using message titles, (2) designing graphical charts, (3) designing concept diagrams, (4) designing text slides, and (5) editing each slide.

1. Using message titles

Every individual slide should have a "message title"—that is, a main heading or "headline" that summarizes the key take-away of that particular slide. The message title should make sense to someone reading it for the first time; put yourself in the shoes of someone who arrived at your presentation late or someone who is reading copies of your slide deck afterwards.

Avoid topic titles. Ineffective presenters use topic titles—that is, titles that simply state the subject of the slide, but don't tell the viewer what message to take away. For example, as visuals guru Gene Zelazny points out in *Say It with Charts*, given the following slide with a topic title only, your audience might perceive any one of the following messages: (1) the number of contracts has increased, (2) the number of contracts is fluctuating, (3) the number of contracts peaked in August, or (4) the number of contracts declined in two of the last eight months.

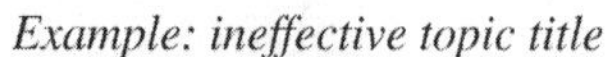

Example: ineffective topic title

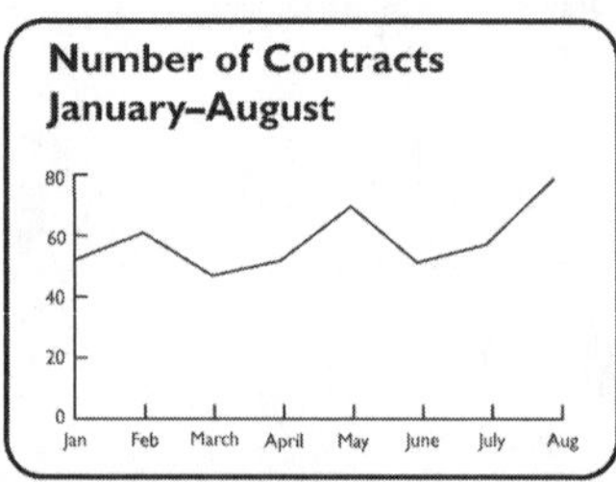

Use a topic title only when you have no message—for example, if you want your audience to discuss trends they observe in the data presented in the slide.

Use message titles. Usually, however, in business presentations, you have a message you want to get across. So make that message clear to your audience by using a message title—that is, a short phrase or sentence with a point to it. Here are some examples:

Ineffective topic titles:	*Effective message titles:*
Company rankings	Company B ranks second.
Web traffic in April	Web traffic dropped off in April
Results	Air quality was the top concern.

Message titles are usually...

- A short phrase or sentence with a point to it, containing a verb or some detail, not just a noun (such as "Comparative Values" or "Rank Order")
- A maximum of 1½ lines long
- Left justified
- Sentence case (as explained on page 115)
- At the top of the slide (not a "kicker" at the end of the slide), as discussed under the direct approach on pages 20–21
- The main idea of your presentation on your agenda and summary slides (not just the topic titles "Agenda" or Summary"), as illustrated on page 107
- One title only (so delete the unnecessary extra heading that appears from Excel)
- Tied to spot color, as explained on page 112

The benefits of message titles include . . .

- *Improve audience comprehension* because they see your main point easily and more quickly
- *Add stand-alone sense* for audience members who come in late or tune out your presentation, and are a useful record for those who read your slide deck later
- *Help you with transitions* because they summarize the main point of the newly shown slide

MESSAGE TITLES AND ACCENT COLOR

1. Accent color alone

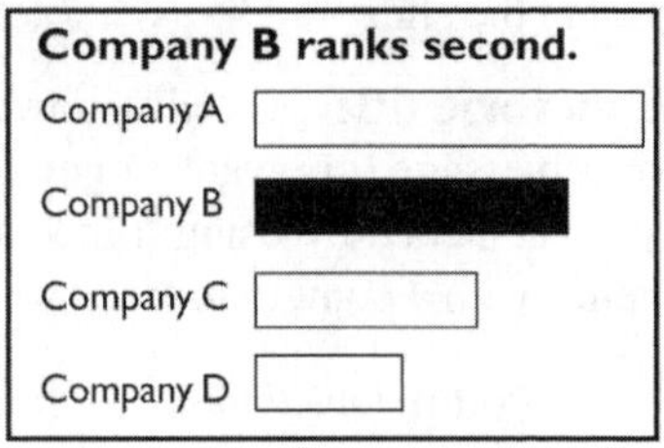

2. With lines

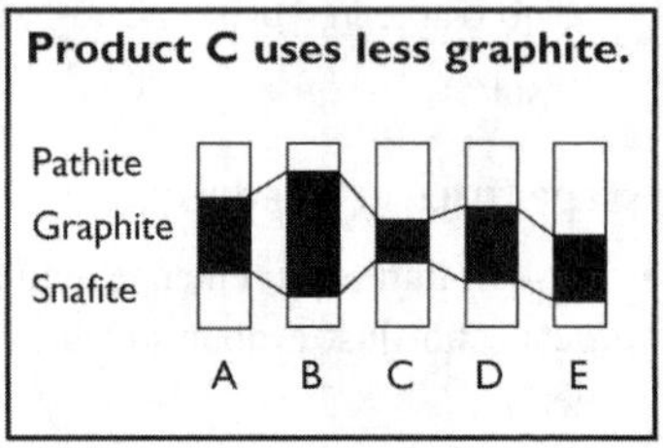

3. With arrows

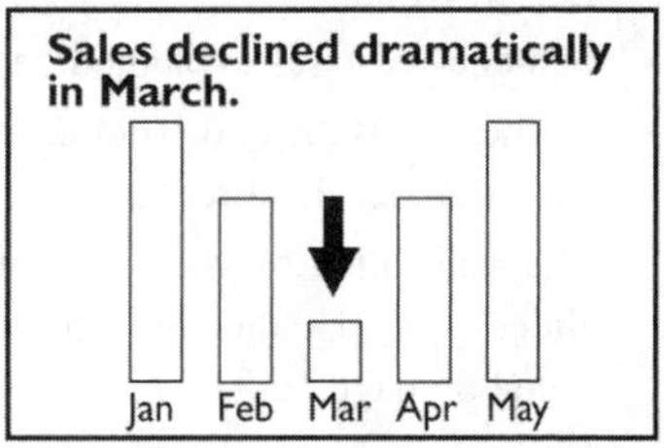

4. With "exploded" off section

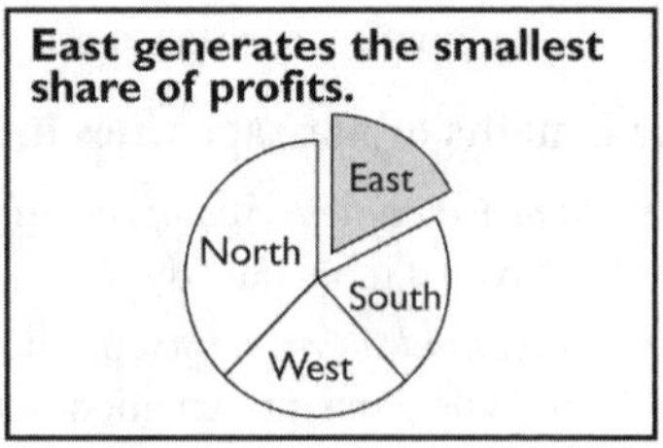

2. Designing graphical charts to show "how much"

Business presentations often include quantitative data—such as financial information, marketing projections, or operations analyses. This kind of information is much easier for your audience to understand and retain if they see it in chart form (e.g., line charts or bar charts) rather being visually assaulted with an on-screen image of an entire spreadsheet, *pro forma* statement, or detailed tabular data. In addition, chart format allows you to highlight your important take-aways from the data much more effectively than pointing to or circling a particular number on a crowded table of numbers. If you do need to show this kind of detailed information, provide it in hard copy.

Examples: table doesn't show trend; graph does

2011		2012	
January	12,543	January	16,985
February	14,371	February	16,106
March	15,998	March	15,422
April	15,004	April	15,010
May	15,281	May	14,564
June	15,742	June	13,820
July	16,101	July	12,489
August	16,254	August	11,376
September	16,378	September	10,897
October	16,495	October	10,178
November	16,397	November	9,657
December	16,463	December	9,281

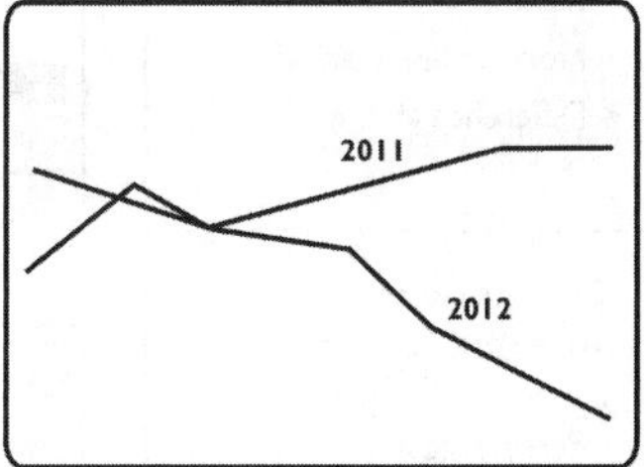

Choose the most effective kind of chart. To show quantitative data graphically, choose from among the most prevalent chart types, shown on the following page. In addition to those shown, other graph types include grouped line chart (with more than one line), grouped bar charts (with more than one bar for each item), sliding bar charts (with a line down the middle of the page and bars on the positive and negative sides), and various other combinations.

Include only relevant data. Keep the following tips in mind before you enter your data on any of the charts shown on the following page.

- *Include only relevant data.* You do not have to include every last bit of data on your charts. Choose only the most important items to insert.
- *Decide on an order* for the individual items (e.g., bars, columns, lines, etc.). Make a conscious choice about ordering them—e.g., high to low or low to high—instead of putting them in random or alphabetical order.

For more details about avoiding prevalent problems with chart design, see pages 124–125 regarding "chartjunk."

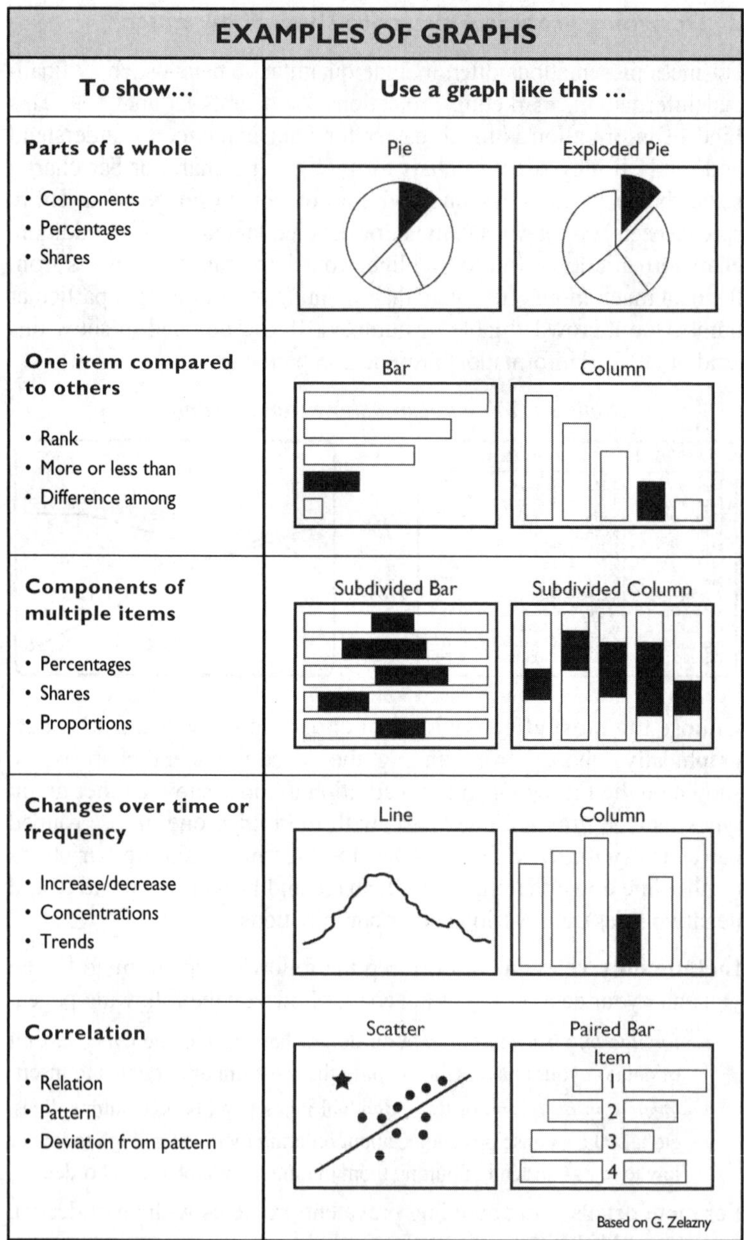

EXAMPLES OF GRAPHS

To show…	Use a graph like this …	
Parts of a whole • Components • Percentages • Shares	Pie	Exploded Pie
One item compared to others • Rank • More or less than • Difference among	Bar	Column
Components of multiple items • Percentages • Shares • Proportions	Subdivided Bar	Subdivided Column
Changes over time or frequency • Increase/decrease • Concentrations • Trends	Line	Column
Correlation • Relation • Pattern • Deviation from pattern	Scatter	Paired Bar Item 1 2 3 4

Based on G. Zelazny

LABELING GRAPHS

1. Preferred option: Label inside section

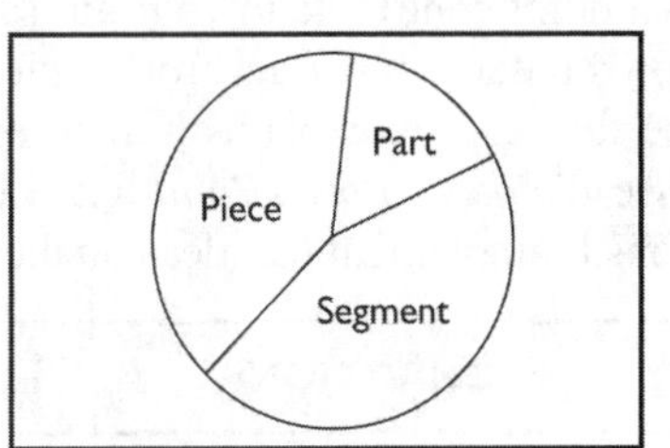

2. Second-best option: Label just outside section

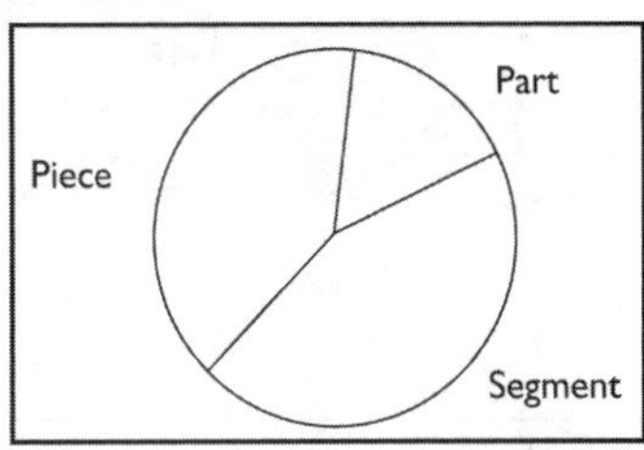

3. Third-best option: Label and connect to section with line

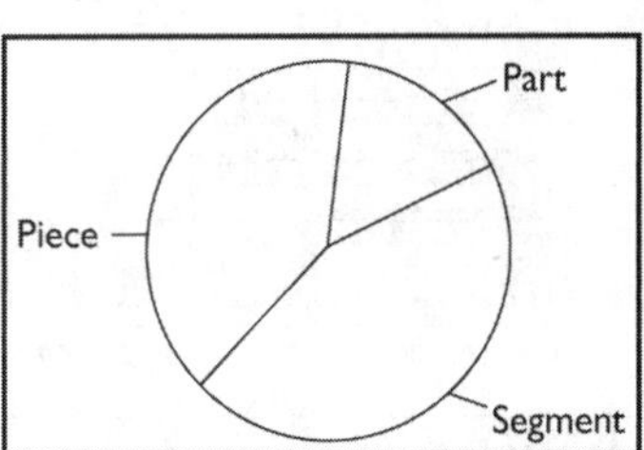

4. Worst option: Use a legend

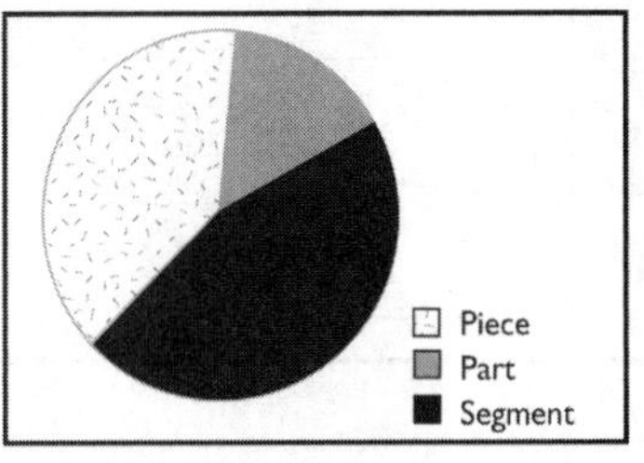

Eliminate chartjunk. To use the term coined by design expert Edward Tufte, eliminate "chartjunk"—those extra design elements that don't contribute to your message. The following examples show how clutter can detract from a pie, bar, and line chart. The table on the facing page explains how to overcome these kinds of problems. (See *Guide to PowerPoint*, cited on page 176, for specific instructions to implement the ideas on the table.)

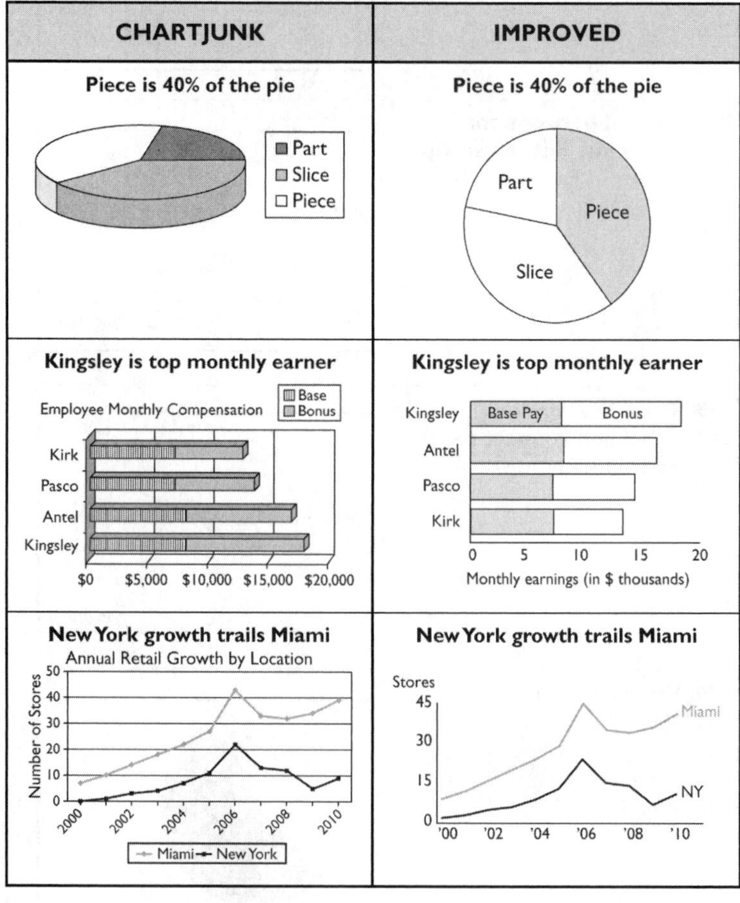

ELIMINATING CHARTJUNK	
Challenge	**Solution**
Legends	Legends slow down the viewer. Instead of using legends, insert labels on the bars, lines, or wedges themselves (as shown in the examples on page 123).
Fruit salad	To avoid the "fruit salad effect" (defined on page 113), delete all of the unnecessary colors and use only the colors that you choose for your Slide Master.
3D views	3D views distort the data (as shown in the example on the previous page), so choose 2D views instead.
Gap width	The "gap width" between each column or each bar should be far less than the width of the column or bar itself. Modify the gap width as necessary to avoid skinny columns or bars.
Complex labels	(1) Eliminate unnecessary extra zeros by adding the word "thousands" or "millions" to the axis label. (2) Remove axis labels altogether if they are unnecessary, e.g., "Years" or "Months." (3) Consider labeling five-year intervals only or omitting every other value to decrease clutter.
Double titles	Delete the extra title that appears when you import a graph from Excel. Use only one message title.
Line chart issues	(1) Increase the line width as necessary to make it more visible. (2) Cut "data markers"—the little squares, triangles, or circles that appear on each line. (3) Avoid fruit salad with lines.
Borders and extra lines	(1) Eliminate the border of background color when it appears around a graph. (2) Cut unnecessary grid lines. (3) Delete the "tick marks" on the axis lines.
Random order	Insert data in an order that reinforces your message title—such as rank order for a bar or column chart or at 12 o'clock for a pie chart.

3. Designing concept diagrams to show "how"

Just as graphical charts help your audience see "how much," concept diagrams help them see "how" your ideas relate to one another. Concept diagrams make the relationship among your ideas visually apparent, add excitement to your slides, and reach the 40% of your audience who are probably visual learners.

Some diagrams illustrate relationships. Diagrams can show how elements interact, parts overlap, items connect, segments relate, and components compare. Here are just a few of the ways you can use them to depict relationships (all of which are illustrated on the facing page):

- *To show interaction,* use connected shapes, like a Venn diagram, which imply overlap. Or you can make one concept part of a larger framework by putting one shape inside another.
- *To emphasize structure,* choose a pyramid diagram if the concepts all build off of the same foundation. Or, if several secondary concepts are linked to one major idea, try a radial or honeycomb layout.
- *To compare concepts,* use a T-chart or two distinct shapes, such as two boxes. For more complex interactions between variables, use a matrix.

Other diagrams highlight sequence. Diagrams can also show the steps in a process, the order of events, and the repetition of stages. Use them to show the following:

- *Linear flow:* To show movement or flow, you might choose arrows, chevrons, or lines. Choose horizontal chevrons to show steps in a process, arrows to show how one idea leads to the next, or an animated line to emphasize movement.
- *Time sequence:* Timelines illustrate events over time. Gantt charts are a type of timeline; they position bars over a timeline to show the starting and stopping points for various stages of a long-term project.
- *Circular flow:* Use circular flow charts only when a cyclical pattern of stages repeats itself continuously—not when the process stops after the final stage.

Make sure concept diagrams make visual sense. Your slides won't make visual sense if you just randomly throw in a few diagrams. Therefore . . .

- *Don't use arrows* unless one idea actually leads to the next.
- *Don't use an overlap diagram* unless the concepts actually overlap.

- *Place ideas of equal importance* on the same horizontal level.
- *Group similar ideas* together visually.
- *Don't use a circular flow diagram* (such as the recycling diagram), unless the last step in the process actually leads back to the first one.

EXAMPLES OF CONCEPT DIAGRAMS		
To show . . .	**. . . use a diagram like one of these:**	
Interaction	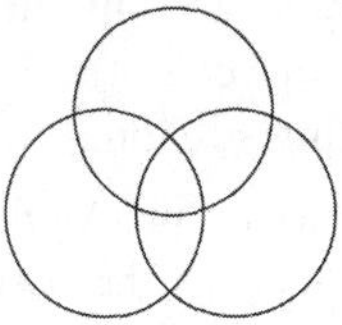 Venn Diagram	 Arrow and Shapes
Structure	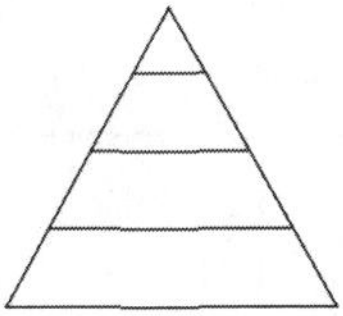 Pyramid Diagram	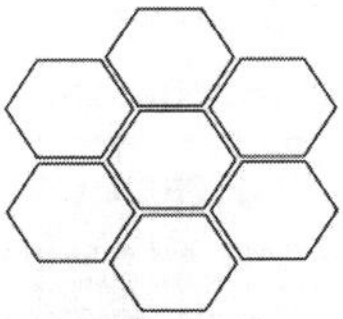 Honeycomb Diagram
Comparison	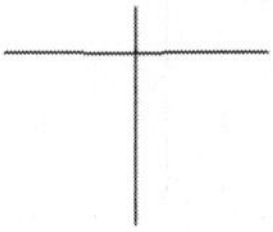 T-Chart	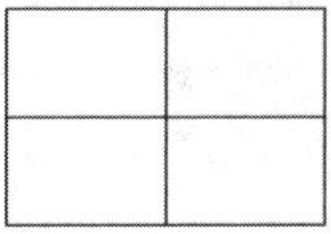 Matrix
Linear flow	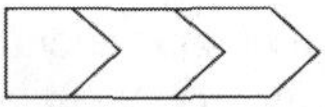 Chevron	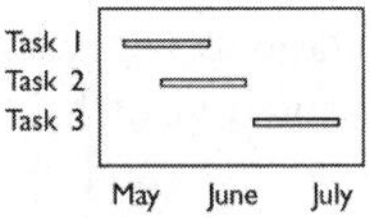 Task 1 Task 2 Task 3 May June July Gantt Chart
Circular flow	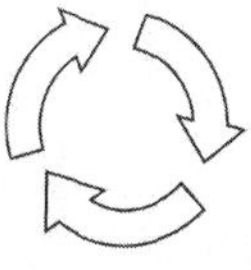 Cycle	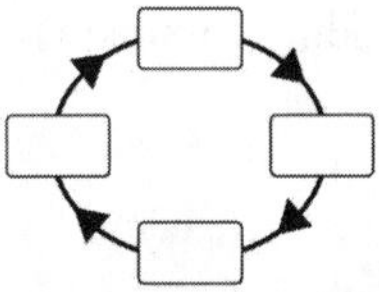 Stages in a Cycle

4. Designing text slides to show "why" or "how"

Avoid overusing text slides that can lead to what Edward Tufte calls "death by bullet list." Instead, use them only to reinforce your main ideas and structure.

Keep text charts simple. Never read your charts word-for-word. Keep your slides exceptionally simple. Deck pages include more information than slides, but still far less than a document. Use the following rules of thumb only as appropriate: break the guideline if necessary, but don't do so on chart after chart—and turn your presentation into a group reading session.

- *For slides:* Aim for the "six by two" guideline—no more than six bullet points per slide and no more than two lines per bullet point.
- *For decks:* Think "ten by three"—no more than ten bullet points on a page and no more than three lines per bullet point.

Ineffective: word-for-word script

INTRODUCTION

Over the past two decades, the waste management industry has undertaken planning as a response to growing markets and an increasingly competitive environment. Understanding historical environmental trends and how they are expected to change is critical to the development of successful strategies of Boford Industries. The purpose of this presentation is to

- Examine the waste management industry today and how it got there
- Assess future trends and their implications
- Discuss how other companies are reacting and changing in response to the external environment

Effective: key ideas only

Presentation Agenda
Boford Industries

- Examine historical trends
- Assess future trends
- Analyze competition

Build lines of text. Since your audience will always read ahead, use animation to focus their attention on your current point. For example, you should virtually always build your agenda slide; it will force you to slow down and help your audience focus on your important points. Also, use animation for any line of text you will be discussing for some time. On the other hand, don't build quick lists where you won't be adding comments to what's on the slide.

Make stand-alone sense. Just like your message titles, your text slides should make comprehensible stand-alone sense to (1) latecomers, (2) someone seeing them for the first time, or (3) someone reading them later.

Ineffective bullet text: Lacks stand-alone sense	*Effective bullet text: Makes stand-alone sense*
• Product	• Unique business model
• Market analysis	• Large market with unmet needs
• Competition	• No direct competition
• Operations	• Institute six-step process

Use telegram language. Pare down your text slides to include key words and phrases only. Use what presentation expert Charlotte Rosen calls "telegram language." In the pre-computer world before the 1980s, people had to communicate urgent messages by telegram, paying for each word they sent and therefore getting rid of all the unnecessary ones.

Ineffective: does not use telegram language

XYZ Corporation has been downgraded by Moody's.

ABC has continued the push for globalization of purchasing.

Effective: uses telegram language

Moody's downgrades XYZ.

ABC pushes for globalized purchasing.

Don't misuse bullet lists. (1) Use bullets for sequence (first to last), priority (most to least, or vice versa), or membership in a set. For any other relationship among your points, use a concept diagram instead. (2) Don't use bullets unless you have at least two bullets to list. (In other words, don't list just one bullet point all by itself.)

Make sure there is more space between each bullet point than within each bullet.

Ineffective spacing between bullets

- Here is a bad example of bullet spacing. As you can see, there is the same amount of space between each bullet as there is within each bullet so the bullets are not differentiated.
- Here is a bad example of bullet spacing. As you can see, there is the same amount of space between each bullet as there is within each bullet so the bullets are not differentiated.

Effective spacing between bullets

- Here is a good example of bullet spacing. As you can see, there is more space between each bullet than there is within each bullet so the bullets are differentiated.

- Here is a good example of bullet spacing. As you can see, there is more space between each bullet than there is within each bullet so the bullets are differentiated.

Check for parallelism. To be clear and consistent, lists need to use parallel structure: (1) *Grammatical parallelism:* The first word of all the items on your list need to use the same grammatical structure (e.g., all start with a verb). (2) *Conceptual parallelism:* Each item should be the same kind of item (e.g., all reasons). (See pages 56 and 164 for more on parallelism.)

Consider your use of case. Most presentations these days use title case and centering for the presentation title only. Message titles and bullet text tend to use sentence case and left justification.

Check your line breaks. Do not automatically accept PowerPoint's line breaks. Instead, override the default line breaks when necessary to avoid (1) *orphans*—that is, one word standing all alone on a line and (2) *ineffective phrase breaks* that break up important phrases.

Ineffective orphan

Combination increases value-added products and
services

Ineffective phrase break

Combination increases value-
added products and services

Effective line break

Combination increases value-added
products and services

5. Using other visual images

PowerPoint offers many other options for enhancing your slides beyond the basic charts, diagrams, and text slides. These enhancements include photographs, drawings, maps, cartoons, video, and audio. (See *Guide to PowerPoint*, cited on page 176, for detailed information on all of these slide enhancements.)

Benefits of other visual images: The options can enhance your presentation because they can…

- *Provide visual variety* to keep the audience's attention,
- *Add a visual aspect* to a text slide,
- *Make a point come alive* in your audience's mind, thereby increasing the likelihood of their remembering your ideas.

Downsides of other visual images: On the other hand, these options can also lead to problems if they send…

- *The wrong message:* If "a picture is worth 1000 words," then the wrong picture will send the wrong 1000 words. Be sure that the picture will increase the impact of your message, not detract from it.
- *An inconsistent message:* Don't leave your audience wondering what your point really is. Don't just toss in an image because it is easy to do so.
- *A confusing message:* Always remember to explain how each image fits into context of what you are discussing.

Possible sources: Be sure you use images legally and cite your sources if appropriate.

- Use photos from PowerPoint clip art.
- Download free photos from the "public domain" such as www.publicdomainsherpa.com or www.morguefile.com.
- Purchase images, for example, from istockphoto.com.

6. Editing each slide

Microedit your visuals just as you would microedit your writing. In addition to editing wordiness by using telegram language, be sure to…

Avoid overload. Avoid overloaded text or graphic visuals that include too much complexity for one chart. If you find yourself with an overloaded visual (such as the example shown at left below), you might choose to (1) simplify it so that the key ideas, figures, or trends are emphasized, as in the example at right, or (2) cut it so that one section is shown in detail, or (3) break it into a series of overlays or progressive "builds," each of which shows an added layer of detail.

Examples: overloaded and simplified

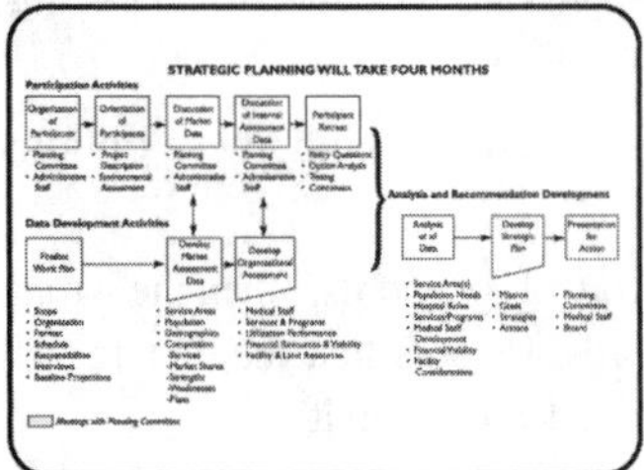

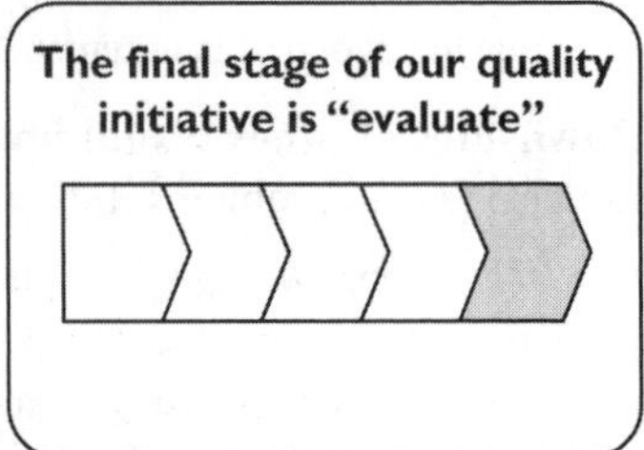

Cite your sources. Document any sources—especially any numbers you use—that come from outside your organization. Citing your sources is not just a matter of correctness and avoiding plagiarism; it is also a way to enhance your credibility.

- *What possible sources*? In addition to just using Wikipedia, consider a multitude of other sources such as www.data.gov, www.worldbank.org, www.Research.stlouisfed/fred 2 (Federal Reserve), www.nber.org/data (National Bureau of Economic Research), www.scholar.google.com, and www.investopedia.
- *How to cite sources?* Follow the conventions used by your audience to decide how much detail to provide and which style guide to use. Typically, on projected visuals, use limited citations, perhaps just nothing but the publication or the author's name. On decks, you can include more detail. You might even want to include a bibliography in an appendix.

Check for errors. Grammar and spelling errors are "credibility killers" on your slides. These kinds of errors are more noticeable and glaring on a large screen in front of a group of people than they are in a printed document. In particular, check for both grammatical and conceptual parallelism, as explained on page 56.

IV. PRACTICING WITH VISUAL AIDS

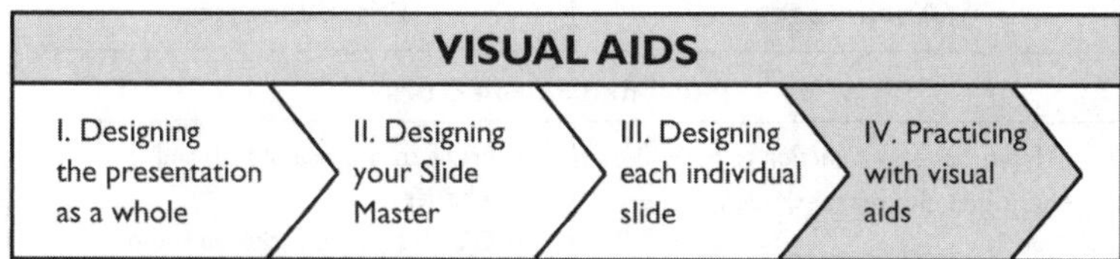

The following sections cover preparation techniques to integrate your visuals gracefully, unobtrusively, and effectively as you speak.

1. General preparation techniques

Here are eight general practice suggestions for using your visuals effectively.

Choose your equipment. Select your equipment based on two sets of issues. (1) *Your audience:* Think about your audience's expectations, size, formality, participation, and need for a permanent record. (2) *Your location:* Also consider the room size and layout, screen size, lighting, and equipment availability. Then, choose your equipment keeping in mind the considerations summarized on the table on the following page.

Familiarize yourself with the equipment. Become extremely comfortable with whatever equipment you have decided to use. Practice until you can use the equipment comfortably, without thinking.

- *Rehearse.* Don't lose credibility by fumbling with your visuals. Instead, practice repeatedly, especially with high-tech options. Practice by interacting with the equipment: actually set it up, turn it on, press the buttons, click the remote, insert the video, flip the pages, position the slides, and so on.
- *Prepare a backup plan.* Think also about what you'll do if your equipment fails. Practice with your backup medium and think about what you will do if equipment trouble eats into your delivery time.

VISUAL AIDS EQUIPMENT	
Advantages	**Disadvantages**
Multimedia projectors	
• Have animation function to build ideas • Can add photographs, video, and/or audio • Can print hard copy of slides • Can be dramatic and even dazzling	• Prone to overuse of bells and whistles • Often require a darkened room • Usually cannot be changed real time • Often intimidate group discussion
Decks and handouts	
• Allow more interaction, bright room lights, and everyone to sit at the same level • Show complex, detailed information • Can be used for audience note-taking and discussion • Provide hard copy: can be distributed before, during, or after the discussion	• Allow audience to read ahead and become distracted from what you are saying • Tend to become overloaded: too many and too complex
Whiteboards and flipcharts	
• Allow for bright room; are good for discussion; can annotate real time; are low tech • *Boards:* unintimidating; good for spontaneity • *Flipcharts:* can attach to walls, provide permanent record	• Too small for large group; cannot show complex images • *Boards:* must erase for more space, often no permanent record • *Flipcharts:* large and clumsy to transport
Overhead projectors	
• Portable, less complex, easy to use • Can annotate real time • Allow easy random access to any slide	• May appear outdated • May block audience's view • Need somewhat darkened room • Lack animation ("build")

Introduce each visual. Think about how you will introduce each new visual to your audience, using the acronym T-MOD to help you remember.

- **T: Transition:** State your backward look/forward look transition (see page 88) while you are displaying either your old slide or your repeated agenda slide (see page 108).
- **M: Message title:** Display the new slide, and then discuss its message title, e.g., "As you can see, the Central American division reached its $6 million goal." Tell your audience why the particular point of this slide matters.
- **O: Orient:** When you are showing complex visuals, introduce the main idea and then explain the meanings of any colors, axes, or symbols you've used. For example, you might say, "Our profits have declined a bit this year, as you can see from this graph. The purple line shows last year's profits and the green line shows this year's." When possible, build complex charts and diagrams (see page 117) so you can provide this kind of explanation as you build the slide.
- **D: Discuss:** Then, your audience will be ready to hear you discuss your bullet points or the take-aways from your graph or diagram.

Cue the audience. Don't assume the audience knows where they are supposed to look. Tell them. Show them. Or do both.

- *Cues for PowerPoint:* One of the advantages of using PowerPoint is the variety of cueing options you have available. For example, you can build each bullet point or each part of a complex chart. Or, you can use bold arrows, boxes, or a contrasting color to cue the audience to look at a particular place on the screen.
- *Cues for decks:* One of the disadvantages of a deck presentation is that your audience can read whatever they want whenever they want. Try to keep them with you by (1) continually referring to page numbers (e.g., "As you can see on page 12") and (2) explaining use of color, axes, symbols, and so on, since you can't use build (e.g., "Note the hiring trend for consulting firms, shown as a blue line.")

Point effectively (with PowerPoint). Take advantage of one of the huge advantages of PowerPoint—its ability to "point" exactly where you want your audience's eyes to focus.

- *Use animation as a "pointer."* Use animation—such as arrows, circles, or other builds—as your PowerPoint "pointer."
- *Do not use the laser pointer* because the dot is tiny and it usually jiggles on the screen.
- *Do not point vaguely* in the direction of the screen.
- *If you want to point on-screen* to a specific bullet point or to a place you hadn't planned to highlight, stand to the left of the screen so you can point at the beginning of each line, rather than to the end of it.
- *Practice with the remote* so you know where it needs to be pointed (often it can be pointed in any direction, so don't make yourself point it exactly toward the screen or monitor). Avoid drawing attention to the remote, especially if you have your notes in the same hand. Practice until you can use it gracefully, instead of aggressively thrusting it with an outreached arm. Some people find it useful to practice by using their cell phone as a substitute for the remote.

Point effectively (with overhead projectors). Pointing when you're using an overhead is problematic. Here are some techniques that work somewhat to get your audience's eyes in the right place.

- *Do not point onto the projector itself* because any nervous shaking will be magnified on-screen. Also avoid pointing by setting a pen or other object on the projector unless you're positive it won't slide around.
- *Use the "revealing lines" technique with caution.* You can use a piece of paper, or better yet cardboard, on the transparency to reveal one line at a time. For some reason, this technique can drive a small percentage of people crazy, evidently because they think you are hiding something from them.
- *Back up to the screen if you point with your hand.* Instead of pointing vaguely in the general vicinity of the screen, if possible, back up to the screen and point to an exact spot on the screen itself.

Don't let your visuals distract the audience.

- *Get rid of "old news."* Once you are done with an image, transition to your next slide, turn over the flipchart, or check with the audience and then erase the board. Don't talk about a new idea while showing an old visual.
- *Avoid empty white screens.* Big, empty, white screens are also distracting. Therefore, if the blank screen would be showing for an exceptionally long time, use the "blank screen" button or insert a plain black slide into your PowerPoint slide show or turn off the overhead projector.

Make eye contact with your audience, not your visuals. Eye contact links you to the audience. They will feel more connected to you and you will be able to read their reactions.

- *Don't be magnetized by your slides.* A common problem with using visuals is that they become "eye-contact magnets"; presenters can't seem to stop looking at them. Therefore, be sure you only glance at your visuals and look at the audience as much as possible.
- *Glance at the screen only briefly.* When a new slide appears, it's fine to glance back at it briefly. But then, turn right back around to face the audience. Including reduced copies of your slides on your notecards (as described on page 90) will also decrease the tendency at the screen too much.
- *Be careful when writing.* Writing on flipcharts and whiteboards is especially challenging for maintaining eye contact. (1) In most *tell/sell presentations*, you should stop talking, write, then look at the audience and discuss what you've written. (2) In *interactive situations*, you may have to write while someone else is speaking, but try to (a) look at the speaker as long as possible before breaking the connection, (b) look back afterward to confirm you got it right, or (c) better yet, use a scribe, as described on pages 96–97.

2. Techniques for specific equipment

In addition to the general advice about visual aids interaction provided in the previous section, here are a few tips for meeting the special challenges inherent in specific kind of equipment.

PowerPoint slide shows

- *Arrive early.* Be sure to arrive early to accomplish three goals. (1) Check your colors on the large screen, modifying them as necessary. What you saw on your computer screen will not be the same as what you will see on the large screen. (2) Set up and test your equipment, especially if you are in a new location or using new equipment. (3) Practice with the remote until you can click it unobtrusively without thrusting it aggressively. Also practice building your points on-screen until it becomes second nature.
- *Select your slide interaction option.* Consider the following four options you may have available. (1) *Use the remote if possible* because it is graceful and unobtrusive and because you can move anywhere you want, without looking down at the keyboard. (2) *Use the keyboard only if necessary* because it restricts your movement and breaks your eye contact. (3) *Do not use the mouse* because the cursor shows (unless you press Ctrl + H). (4) *Do not use the laser pointer* because the dot is tiny and usually jiggles on the screen.

Decks and handouts

- *Assume people will read* whatever is in front of them. Therefore, try to control when to distribute hard copy: (1) *In advance:* general handouts (such as the agenda), handouts intended for note-taking, or decks intended to be read in advance. (2) *When you are discussing:* complex information or detailed handouts only at the exact time when you are discussing them. (3) *At the end:* detailed summaries or leave-behinds.
- *Explain the deck's purpose* and how you will be using it as you speak.
- *Maintain eye contact* with the audience to encourage them not to lag behind or jump ahead in the deck.
- *Cue people* by referring to the page numbers on the deck.
- *Don't read the deck.* Talk to the audience, not word-for-word from the paper. If possible, place the deck on the table so you can gesture, and be sure to look up so you can make eye contact.
- *Remember that bound decks* are easier to flip than those that are stapled.

Overheads

- *Check your equipment.* Know where the spare bulb is and either learn how to install it or else arrange for a backup projector. Also, be sure you have the right kind of marking pens—not flipchart markers or regular pens.
- *Make sure everyone can see the screen.* (1) Check to see if the projector or projector arm is blocking anybody's view. (2) Then, avoid standing next to the projector where you may also block someone's view; instead, stand back flush with the screen, so you can cue the audience by pointing on it. (3) Finally, avoid walking too often between the screen and the projector when the projector is turned on.
- *Frame your overheads* so they are easier to handle and block the extra light around the transparency; unframed overheads stick together and are harder to place straight on the projector. You might also try putting a piece of masking tape across the bottom of the projector's screen to help you line up your overheads evenly.

Flipcharts

- *Use thick markers* and highly visible colors (e.g., black, blue, and green; not orange or yellow). Check the markers in advance and keep spares nearby.
- *Write the message headings* in advance to save time while you are talking.
- *Practice flipping pages* over when you are done with them.
- *Leave a blank page* between used pages. You will be able to flip each page more easily if, in advance, you turn up the bottom corner of each page together with its following blank page.
- *Bring masking tape* if you want to post pages around the room. Or, even better, use a pad of the flipchart-sized sticky notes.
- *Practice with your scribe.* If you choose to work with a scribe (as recommended on page 96), make it clear in advance how you will work together; instruct him or her to write either (1) only the phrases you indicate or (2) wording at his or her discretion.

Besides your visual aids (covered in this chapter), think about your presentation structure (Chapter V) and nonverbal delivery (Chapter VII). The checklist on page 158 summarizes all three of these sets of speaking skills.

CHAPTER VII OUTLINE

I. Nonverbal delivery skills
   1. Body language
   2. Vocal traits
   3. Space and objects
   4. Practice and arrangements
   5. Physical relaxation
   6. Mental relaxation
   7. Last-minute relaxation

II. Nonverbal listening skills
   1. Attending skills
   2. Encouraging skills
   3. Following skills

CHAPTER VII

Speaking: Nonverbal Skills

Your words (Chapter V) and your visual aids (Chapter VI) make up only a portion of what you communicate. In fact, experts estimate that 60%–90% of what you communicate is nonverbal. This chapter covers those nonverbal messages you send—the way you appear and sound to others.

The first part of the chapter covers those nonverbal messages you send in a tell/sell presentation—the way you appear and sound. The second part concentrates on the nonverbal listening skills to use in various interactive consult/join situations. The examples in this chapter are based on U.S. business practices; keep in mind that nonverbal communication varies widely across different cultures, as discussed on pages 29–31.

NONVERBAL SKILLS		
Section in this chapter	**I. Nonverbal Delivery Skills**	**II. Nonverbal Listening Skills**
Who speaks most	You	Your audience
Purposes	To inform or to persuade	To understand
Typical situations	Tell/sell presentations	Questions and answers Consult/join meetings One-to-one conversations

I. NONVERBAL DELIVERY SKILLS

NONVERBAL SKILLS		
Section in this chapter	**I. Nonverbal Delivery Skills**	**II. Nonverbal Listening Skills**
Who speaks most	You	Your audience
Purposes	To inform or to persuade	To understand
Typical situations	Tell/sell presentations	Questions and answers Consult/join meetings One-to-one conversations

Nonverbal delivery skills include not only body language but also vocal traits (that is, how you sound, not what you say) and the use of space and objects around you. The analysis of each of these skills will be followed by techniques you can use to improve them.

1. Body language

Keep in mind the following five elements of body language.

Posture: Effective speakers exhibit poise through their posture.

- Stand in a relaxed, professional manner—comfortably upright, squarely facing your audience, with your weight balanced and distributed evenly. Your feet should be aligned under your shoulders—neither too close nor too far apart.
- Watch out for (1) rocking, swaying, or bouncing; (2) leaning, slouching, or the "hip sit/parking on your hip"; (3) "frozen" poses such as the stiff "Attention!" or the wide-legged "cowpoke straddle" stances.

Body movement: You do not have to stand stock-still or plan every move artificially. Instead . . .

- Move with a purpose. For example, walk to the other side of the room after you've completed a main section or every five minutes or so, or step forward to emphasize a point.
- Avoid random, constant, repetitive, or purposeless motion—such as pacing or rocking.

Hand and arm gestures: Effective speakers use their hands the same way they would in conversation.

- Discover your natural style, letting your hands do whatever they would be doing if you were speaking to one person instead of to a group. Be yourself: some people use expansive gestures; others are more reserved. For example, let your hands move conversationally, be still for a while, emphasize a point, or describe an object.
- Avoid putting your hands in any one position and leaving them there without change—such as the "fig leaf" (hands clasped in front), the "parade rest" (hands clasped in back), the "gunshot wound" (hand clutching opposite arm), or the "commander" (hands on hips). Avoid nervous-looking gestures, such as ear-tugging or arm-scratching. Finally, avoid "authority killers" like flipping your hair or waving your arms randomly.

Facial expression: Your facial expression should also look natural, as it would in conversation.

- Keep your face relaxed to look interested and animated. Vary your expression according to the subject and the occasion.
- Avoid a stony, deadpan expression; also, avoid inappropriate facial expression, such as smiling when you are talking about something sad or negative.

Eye contact: Eye contact is a crucial nonverbal skill. It makes possible what communication expert Lynn Russell calls the "listener/speaker connection": the audience feels connected with you and you feel connected with them and can read their reactions.

- Start by looking at the friendly faces. Then connect with other people throughout the room long enough to complete a sentence. You don't need to keep 100% eye contact; you may need to look up (not down) briefly to think. If, after your presentation, you can remember what the people in your audience looked like, you had good eye contact.
- Avoid looking continually at your notes, the screen, the ceiling, or the floor. Don't show a preference for looking at one side of the room or the other. Finally, avoid fake eye contact—such as "eye dart" (eyes moving quickly or randomly) or "lighthouse scan" (glossed-over eyes moving back-and-forth across the room).

2. Vocal traits

Body language (how you look) is only one aspect of nonverbal skills. Vocal traits (how you sound) are equally important for establishing credibility. Vocal traits are based on how you say it, not on what you say. See page 149 for vocal relaxation exercises.

Intonation: Intonation refers to the modulation, pitch, variation, and inflection in your voice.

- *Do speak* with expression and enthusiasm, sounding natural and interesting, with variety in your pitch.
- *Do not speak* in a dull, robotic, bored-sounding monotone. Watch out for "voice uplift" (ending sentences as if they were questions) that makes you sound tentative and unsure of yourself.

Volume: Your volume is determined by how loudly or softly you speak. Remember to (1) speak loudly enough to be heard by the people in the back row of the room, (2) vary your volume to add interest, (3) watch out for "volume fade" at the ends of your sentences.

Rate: Rate is the speed with which you speak. Don't bore your audience with an overly slow rate or lose them with an overly fast one. Since you probably cannot judge your own rate, ask a colleague or friend to assess it for you. A good way to slow down your rate is to use more pauses (followed by an in-breath) at the end of your sentences and before or after important points. Remember to slow down especially if you have an unfamiliar accent or if you are speaking to non-native audience members.

Fillers: Fillers are verbal pauses—like *uh*, *um*, and *y'know*.

- *Try to become comfortable pausing* during your presentation to collect your thoughts. The pause, which may sound interminably long to you, is most likely imperceptible to your audience—so you don't need to fill it up with a sound.
- *Don't obsess* if you notice a few fillers; everybody uses them occasionally. Instead, aim to avoid the distracting, habitual overuse of fillers.

Enunciation: Enunciation refers to how clearly you articulate your words. Pronounce your words clearly and crisply. Avoid the following, all of which may be perceived as sounding uneducated or sloppy: mumbling, squeezing words together (as in *gonna* or *wanna*), leaving out syllables (as in *guvmint*), and dropping final consonants (as in *thousan'* or *goin'*).

3. Space and objects

Another component of nonverbal communication is the use of space and objects around you. Objects and space affect four sets of choices: seating arrangements, speaker height and distance, use of objects, and dress.

Seating: The way you arrange the chairs for a presentation will communicate nonverbally what kind of interaction you want to have with your audience. Choose straight lines of chairs for the least interactive sessions. Choose horseshoe-shaped or u-shaped lines of chairs to encourage more interaction. For smaller groups, choose either (1) a rectangular table (seating yourself at the head to emphasize your leadership or on the side to signal equality among the participants) or (2) a round table to show even more equality.

Height and distance: The higher you are in relation to your audience, the more formal the atmosphere you are establishing nonverbally. Therefore, the most formal presentations might be delivered from a stage or a platform. In a semiformal situation, you stand while your audience sits. To make the situation even less formal, place yourself and your audience at the same level: sit together around a table or seat yourself in front of the group. Similarly, the closer you are, the less formal you appear.

Objects: The more objects you place between yourself and the audience, the more formal the interaction. To increase formality, use a podium, desk, or table between yourself and the audience. To decrease formality, stand or sit without any articles of furniture between you and your audience.

Dress: What you wear also communicates something to your audience. Dress to project the image that you want to create, the one that will establish your credibility. Dress appropriately for the audience, the occasion, the organization, and the culture. For instance, what is appropriate in the fashion industry may be totally inappropriate in the banking industry. Finally, don't wear clothes that will distract from what you are saying—such as exaggerated, dangling jewelry or a loud, flashy tie.

4. Practice and arrangements

Using the following practice and arrangement techniques will improve your nonverbal delivery significantly.

Practice techniques: Here are some possible practice techniques.

- *Avoid reading or memorizing.* You won't be able to establish eye contact or rapport if you are reading. Nor will you have time to memorize every presentation you ever make. Instead, practice speaking conversationally, referring to your notes (explained on page 90) as little as possible.
- *Rehearse out loud and on your feet.* Knowing your content and saying it aloud are two completely different activities, so do not practice by sitting down and silently reading your notes. Instead, practice out loud and on your feet. For an important presentation, rehearse the entire thing aloud. For a less important presentation, at least practice the opening, closing, and main transitions this way.
- *Memorize three key parts.* Another suggestion is to memorize your opening, closing, and major transitions. These are the times when speakers feel the most nervous and are most apt to lose composure.
- *Concentrate on your introduction.* A strong introduction will make a positive first impression and will make you feel more comfortable at the beginning of your presentation, when you are likely to feel nervous.
- *Practice with your visuals* as discussed on pages 133–139.
- *Improve your delivery.* While you're practicing, you can work to improve your delivery by (1) recording your rehearsal, (2) practicing in front of a friend or a colleague, or (3) speaking into a mirror to improve your facial expression or into an audiotape recorder to improve your vocal expression.
- *Simulate the situation.* You might try practicing in the actual place where you will be making the presentation or in front of chairs set up as they will be when you speak.
- *Time yourself.* Time yourself in advance to avoid the irritating problem of running overtime during your presentation. You prefer short presentations; so does your audience. During your rehearsal, remember to (1) speak slowly, as you would to actual people, rather than just reading through your ideas; (2) speak extra slowly during your preview, to give the audience enough time to digest it; (3) include time for changing and explaining your slides; and (4) budget some time for interruptions and questions. Limit yourself to 80% of the allotted time when you're rehearsing; the real presentation virtually always runs 20% longer than the practice session.

Arrangement reminders: Another way to gain confidence is to make the necessary arrangements for your presentation so that you won't be flustered upon discovering your computer doesn't work or you have too few chairs. All the work you do to create a presentation may be wasted if you haven't dealt with these arrangements. Remember that you are responsible for your own arrangements. Although the janitor, your secretary, or the audiovisual technician can help you out, you are the one who will be suffering in front of the audience if things go awry.

You will deliver your presentation more effectively if you arrive 20 to 30 minutes early to check the arrangements, fix anything that may be wrong, get comfortable with the place, and mingle with the audience.

- *Room:* First, double-check your room arrangements. Make sure that you have enough chairs, but not too many. Get rid of extras in advance; people don't like to move once they're seated. Make sure that the chairs are arranged as you want them and that any other items you ordered are there and functioning. Check the lighting, ventilation, sources of noise, and any other potential distractions. (If, despite your best efforts, a distraction occurs during the presentation, don't get flustered or pretend it's not happening. Deal with it as naturally as you can).
- *Visual aids:* Second, check your visual aids. Make sure that all the equipment and accessories you ordered have arrived. Test all the equipment far enough in advance so that you can get someone to fix or replace it if necessary. Get the number to call if something should break down during your presentation. Test the readability (such as font size and color contrast) of your slides by viewing them from the farthest chair or asking someone seated in the back row. Make sure that every person in the audience will be able to see your visuals. Finally, check the sequence of your slides and handouts.
- *Yourself:* Finally, arrange yourself (as it were). Set up your notes and anything else you might need, such as a glass of water. Remember that you are "on stage" from the moment the first person arrives. Prepare yourself physically and mentally by using one of the specific relaxation techniques described on the following six pages.

5. Physical relaxation

When speaking in front of a group, most people feel a surge of adrenaline. In fact, fear of public speaking ranks as Americans' number one fear—ahead of both death and loneliness. Although most people experience this burst of adrenaline, the trick is to get that energy working for you, instead of against you, by finding an effective relaxation technique. Experiment with the various methods explained on the next six pages until you find the one or two techniques that are most useful for you.

The first set of relaxation techniques is based on the assumption, shared by many performers and athletes, that by relaxing yourself physically, you will calm yourself mentally.

Exercise. One way to channel your nervous energy is to exercise before you present. Many people find that the physical exertion of running, working out, or other such athletic activities calms them down.

Try progressive relaxation. Developed by psychologist Edmund Jacobson, this technique involves tensing and relaxing muscle groups. To practice this technique, set aside about 10 or 15 minutes of undisturbed time in a comfortable, darkened place where you can lie down. Tense (by clenching vigorously for five to seven seconds) and relax (by releasing and enjoying the feeling for at least 10 seconds) each muscle group in turn: face, neck and chest, arms and hands, chest and upper back, stomach and lower back, upper legs, lower legs, and feet. Repeat the procedure at least twice.

Breathe deeply. For at least one full minute, sit or lie on your back with your hand on your diaphragm, at the bottom half of your rib cage. Both of the following techniques emphasize the out breath, because it is the calming one.

- *Yoga "sigh breath":* Inhale slowly through your nose to the count of four, feeling your diaphragm expand. Exhale even more slowly through your mouth feeling your diaphragm empty—to the count of six to eight, or counting backwards from four—and sighing aloud.
- *Sarnoff squeeze:* Similarly, speech coach Dorothy Sarnoff recommends inhaling through your nose and exhaling through your mouth, making a "sssss" sound and contracting the abdominus rectus muscles, what she calls the "vital triangle" just below the rib cage.

Relax specific body parts. For some people, stage fright manifests itself in certain parts of the body—for example, tensed shoulders, quivering arms, or fidgety hands. Here are some exercises to relax specific body parts.

- *Neck and throat:* Gently roll your neck from side to side, front to back, chin to chest, or all the way around.
- *Shoulders:* Raise one or both shoulders as if you were shrugging. Then roll them back, then down, then forward. After several repetitions, rotate in the opposite direction.
- *Arms:* Shake out your arms, first only at the shoulders, then only at the elbow, finally letting your hands flop at the wrist.
- *Hands:* Repeatedly clench and relax your fists. Start with an open hand and close each finger one by one to make a fist; hold the clench; then release.
- *Face:* Close your eyes and wiggle your face muscles: forehead, nose, cheeks, and jaws. Move your jaw side-to-side.

Prepare your voice. Some nervous symptoms affect your voice—such as quivering, dry mouth, or sounding out-of-breath. Here are some general suggestions for keeping your voice in shape:

- *Be awake and rested.* Get enough sleep the night before your presentation, so your voice will be rested. Wake up several hours before your presentation to provide a natural warm-up period for your voice.
- *Take a hot shower.* A hot shower will wake up your voice; the steam will soothe a tired or irritated set of vocal cords.
- *Drink warm liquids.* Ideal candidates are herbal tea or warm water with lemon. Warm liquids with caffeine are fine for your voice, but they might increase your heart rate.
- *Avoid consuming milk* or other dairy products. Dairy products tend to coat the vocal cords, which may cause problems during your presentation.
- *Avoid dry mouth* by (1) sucking a cough drop or hard candy, (2) chewing gum, or (3) biting your tongue before the presentation.
- *Warm up your vocal cords* by humming, repeating vowels, or singing. Start slowly and quietly, gradually adding volume and a full range of pitches.
- *During the presentation:* (1) *Drink water:* Keep water nearby. If you have dry mouth, pause and drink as needed. (2) *Breathe deeply* from the diaphragm (below the rib cage), not shallowly from the shoulders or upper chest.

6. Mental relaxation

Some speakers prefer mental relaxation techniques— to control physical sensation mentally. Here are various mental relaxation techniques to try until you find one that works for you.

Think positively. (1) Base your thinking on the Dale Carnegie argument: "To feel brave, act as if you are brave. To feel confident, act as if you are confident." (2) Repeat positive words or phrases, such as "poised, perfect, prepared, poised, perfect, prepared." (3) Use positive labeling such as "I'm excited" rather than "I'm scared."

Think nonjudgmentally. Describe your behavior ("I notice a monotone") rather than judging it ("I have a terrible speaking voice!"). Then change the behavior through rational thinking or positive self-imagery, both of which are described below.

Think rationally. Avoid becoming trapped in the "ABCs of emotional reactions," as developed by psychologist Albert Ellis. **A** stands for the "activating event" (such as catching yourself using a filler word), which sparks an irrational **B** or "belief system" (such as "I must be absolutely perfect in every way; if I'm not perfect, then I must be terrible"), which causes **C** or "consequences" (such as anxiety or depression). Ellis recommends **D** or "disputing" these ABCs with a rational thought (such as "I don't demand absolute perfection from other speakers" or "Using one filler word is not the end of the world. I'll go on naturally instead of getting flustered.")

Use a positive self-image. Many speakers find that positive self-pictures work better than positive words.

- *Visualize yourself as successful.* Visualize yourself hearing positive comments or applause. Then act out the role of the person you visualized.
- *Use a positive DVD picture.* Using a DVD or video of yourself speaking, freeze the frame at a point where you look effective. During your next presentation, visualize and then recreate that person.
- *Think of yourself as the guru.* Remind yourself that you know your subject matter.
- *Put yourself "in character"* of a good speaker by your comportment and dress.

Don't think. (1) *While you are waiting to speak,* fill your mind with something mindless, like saying the alphabet. (2) *While you are speaking,* turn off your internal self-analysis and don't think about how you look or sound.

Try visualization. Relax by conjuring up in your mind a visual image of a positive and pleasant object or scene.

- *Imagine a scene.* On each of the several days before the presentation, close your eyes and imagine a beautiful, calm scene, such as a beach you have visited. Imagine the details of temperature, color, and fragrance. If your mind wanders, bring it back to your scene. Concentrate on the image and exclude all else. Try repeating positive phrases, such as "I feel warm and relaxed" or "I feel content."
- *Juxtapose the stress.* A few days before the presentation, visualize the room, the people, and the stresses of the presentation. Then distance yourself and relax by visualizing the pleasant image. This technique decreases stress by defusing the situation in your mind.

Connect with the audience. Try to see your audience as real people.

- *Meet them and greet them.* When people are arriving, greet them and get to know some of them. Then, when you're speaking, find those people in the audience and try to feel as if you are having a one-to-one conversation with them.
- *Remember they are individuals.* Even if you can't greet the people in the audience, think of them as individual people, not as an amorphous audience. As you speak, imagine you are conversing with them.
- *Imagine you are speaking to a friend,* not to a group.
- *"Befriend" the audience.* Picture yourself in your own home, enthusiastically talking with old friends. Try to maintain a sense of warmth and goodwill. This altered perception can not only diffuse your anxiety, but also increase your positive energy.

Transform negative to positive. Consider the adrenaline that may be causing nervous symptoms as positive energy. All speakers may feel butterflies in their stomachs; effective speakers get those butterflies to fly in formation—thereby transforming negative energy into positive energy.

7. Last-minute relaxation

When it's actually time to deliver the presentation, here are a few relaxation techniques that you can use at the last minute—and even as you speak.

Manage your physical symptoms. Obviously, you can't start doing push-ups or practice humming when you are in the room waiting to present. Fortunately, there are a few subtle techniques you can use at the last minute to relax your body and your voice:

- *Try isometric exercise.* These quick exercises can be used discreetly to steady shaking hands or prevent tapping feet. Isometric exercises involve clenching and then quickly relaxing your muscles. For example you might (1) clench and release your hands (behind your back or under the table) or (2) clench, release, press, or wiggle your feet against the floor.
- *Take a deep breath.* Inhale slowly and deeply. Exhale completely. Imagine you are breathing in "the good" and out "the bad." A deep breath can slow your heart rate. Also use it to remind yourself that pausing gives you a chance to take in all the air your voice will need to make sound effectively.
- *Sip water.* If you suffer from a dry mouth, drink some water before you start to present. Also, have water available as you speak so you can pause and take a sip as needed.

Improve your mental state. Also, at the last minute, you can dispel stage fright by using what psychologists call "internal dialogue," which means, of course, talking to yourself. Here are some of the messages you may want to generate:

- *Give yourself a pep talk.* Act like a coach and deliver motivational messages to yourself, such as "I'm prepared and ready to do a great job. My slides are first-rate. I can answer any question that comes my way."
- *Play up the audience's reception.* Look at the audience and find something positive to say about them: "These people are really going to be interested in what I have to say" or "They seem like a very friendly group."
- *Repeat positive phrases.* Develop an internal mantra that can help you overcome your fears, such as "I know my stuff; I know my stuff" or "I'm glad I'm here; I'm glad I'm here."

Relax as you speak. Finally, here are five techniques you can use to relax even as you speak.

- *Speak to the "motivational listeners."* There are always a few kind souls out there who are nodding, smiling, and generally reacting favorably. Especially at the beginning of your presentation, look at them, not at the people reading, looking out the window, or yawning. Looking at the positive listeners will increase your confidence; soon, you will be looking at the people around those good listeners and ultimately at every person in the audience.
- *Talk to someone in the back.* To make sure your voice sounds strong and confident, take a deep breath and talk to someone sitting in the back. Try to maintain this audible volume throughout your talk.
- *Remember that you probably look better than you think you do.* Your nervousness is probably not as apparent to your audience as it is to you. Experiments show that even trained speech instructors do not see all of the nervous symptoms speakers think they are exhibiting. Managers and students watching recordings of their performances regularly say, "Hey, I look better than I thought I would!"
- *Forget about how you look and sound* while you're speaking. Ignore any stumbles or mistakes. Don't apologize or confess your nervousness.
- *Concentrate on the here and now.* Focus on your ideas and your audience. Forget about past regrets and future uncertainties. You have already analyzed what to do; now just do it wholeheartedly. Enjoy communicating your information to your audience, and let your enthusiasm show.

II. NONVERBAL LISTENING SKILLS

NONVERBAL SKILLS		
Section in this chapter	**I. Nonverbal Delivery Skills**	**II. Nonverbal Listening Skills**
Who speaks most	You	Your audience
Purposes	To inform or to persuade	To understand
Typical situations	Tell/sell presentations	Questions and answers Consult/join meetings One-to-one conversations

In the first part of this chapter, we looked at nonverbal delivery skills to use when delivering a presentation. In this second section, we will consider a second set of nonverbal skills: the nonverbal listening skills to use in interactive situations.

Various studies show that businesspeople spend 45%–63% of their time listening, yet as much as 75% of what gets said is ignored, misunderstood, or forgotten. Why? In part, because most of us have had little or no training in listening; because we can think at least four times faster than someone can talk; and because sometimes it's hard to avoid jumping to conclusions or becoming defensive before we've heard the other person out.

By learning to listen well, you will not only receive and retain better information, but you will also (1) be more persuasive because you will satisfy your audience's desire to be heard and (2) improve both your rapport and your audience's morale.

The following advice for improving listening skills is adapted from listening expert Robert Bolton. The three listening skills clusters include (1) attending skills, (2) encouraging skills, and (3) following skills. (For much more information about listening and one-to-one communication, see the *Guide to Interpersonal Communication*, cited on page 175.)

1. Attending skills

The term "attending skills" means giving physical attention to the speaker—"listening" with your body—either one-on-one or with a group. Like all nonverbal skills, these techniques will, of course, vary in different cultures.

Posture of involvement: To look involved, your posture should look relaxed, yet alert. Maintain an open position, with your arms uncrossed. Do not stay rigid or unmoving; move in response to what the speaker is saying. When seated, lean forward toward the speaker, facing her or him squarely. Another way to show interest nonverbally is to mirror the same degree of formality in your posture as the other person is using.

Eye contact: Eye contact also signals your interest and involvement. Maintain steady, comfortable eye contact for a few seconds, then gaze around the speaker's face to "read" his or her expression, and then back to the eyes. Do not glance toward distant objects, which signals noninterest. Avoid such obvious signs of rudeness as looking at your watch or gazing out the window.

Distance: Sit or stand at the appropriate distance from the speaker—neither too close nor too far apart. Cross-cultural expert Edward Hall has identified zones of space in the U.S. culture: such as 18 inches to 4 feet is "personal space," while 0 to 18 inches is "intimate space." But perhaps the best way to judge distance is by being aware of your audience's comfort level: if the other person is leaning away, you're too close; if leaning toward you, you may be too far away. Another way to signal your willingness to listen is to avoid standing or sitting at a higher level than the other person. When seated, remember that (1) the head of the table is associated with dominance and (2) sitting beside someone may be perceived as cooperative, while sitting across from someone may be perceived as competitive.

Eliminating barriers: To give your undivided attention, try to remove any possible distractions. In your office, for example, you might have your calls held, close your door, and come out from behind your desk. In a group situation, you might come out from behind the table or podium. In addition, remove any mental barriers such as thinking about other tasks, making plans, or daydreaming.

2. Encouraging skills

In addition to using nonverbal attending skills, use the following three "encouraging skills" to let the other person speak and to avoid speaking too much yourself.

Open-ended questions: One of the main ways to get people to talk is to ask them effective questions. The questions designed to elicit the most information from others are known as "open-ended questions"—that is, questions that cannot be easily answered with a "yes" or "no." For example, you are likely to get more extensive responses if you . . .

Ask . . .	**Instead of . . .**
Tell me about the computer project.	Is the computer project going well?
What concerns you about the deadlines on this schedule?	Can you meet the deadlines on this schedule?
How shall we solve this problem?	Do you like my solution?

Door openers: "Door openers" are nonjudgmental, reassuring ways of inviting other people to speak if they want to. For example, "All right. Let's hear what the rest of you have to say about this" or "You look upset. Care to talk about it?" In contrast, typical door closers include the following:

- *Criticizing:* "You get all upset no matter what we do!"
- *Advising:* "I was upset when I first heard of this too, but all you have to keep in mind is . . ."
- *Overusing logic:* "I don't see what you have to look so upset about. These numbers speak for themselves . . ."
- *Reassuring:* "Don't worry; I'm sure you'll understand after you hear . . ."
- *Stage-hogging:* Responding to someone else's story by telling one of your own. Even if you are trying to show understanding, they will often feel one-upped.

Attentive silence and encouragers: Perhaps the hardest listening skill of all is simply to stop talking. Effective listeners must learn to be comfortable with appropriate silence. Silence gives the other person time to think and to set the pace. Hear the speaker out, even if the message is unwelcome. Instead of talking or interrupting, show your interest by nodding your head and using "minimal encouragers," such as "I see," "Yes," or "Uh-huh."

3. Following skills

Paraphrasing content: Paraphrasing means restating the other person's ideas accurately and concisely. Using this skill will enable you to check the accuracy of what you think you have heard, encourage the other person to elaborate on what she or he has said, and show that you are listening. Listen for main ideas, patterns, and themes, and organize those main thoughts as you listen—rather than judging or evaluating first. Then restate a few key words or summarize the key thoughts or idea. For example, "So, it sounds as if you are making three suggestions . . ." then list them or "Seems as though your major concern here is . . ."

Paraphrasing feelings: In addition to hearing what the person says, be sensitive to how he or she says it. Listen "between the lines." Be aware of the speaker's tone of voice, volume, facial expression, and body movement. Examples of paraphrased feelings include "You sound upset about the new policy" or "You seem discouraged about the way your team is getting along" or "Looks like you're pleased with those results."

Note-taking or recording: You may wish to take notes as you listen to show that you are really interested and planning to follow up. In one-to-one situations, explain why you are taking notes; limit yourself to very few notes so you don't lose your sense of connection; and consider sharing the notes as a summary. Sometimes, however, note-taking may be inappropriate. Gauge the situation to determine whether taking notes will make the speaker feel policed or whether you will concentrate too much on writing. Sometimes, showing your concern with full eye contact is more important than recording the facts. In a group situation, however, it's usually helpful to record participant comments (either by yourself or with a scribe, as described on page 96.)

See the checklists on the following pages for a summary of all the skills covered in the speaking half of the book: *tell/sell presentations* (structure, visuals, and nonverbal delivery) and *consult/join meetings* (what you say and nonverbal listening skills). For much more detail on these two sets of skills, see (1) *Guide to Presentations* and (2) *Guide to Meetings*, both cited on page 176.

TELL/SELL PRESENTATION CHECKLIST

1. Verbal structure: what you say
Chapter V

1. Was your presentation structured effectively (opening, preview, clear main points, closing)?
2. Did you prepare an outline with key phrases only?
3. Did you prepare how and when to take questions?

2. Visual aids: what your audience sees
Chapter VI

1. Did you design your presentation as a whole (turn structure into slides, tie slides together)?
2. Did you design your Slide Master (colors, fonts, animation)?
3. Did you design each individual slide (message titles, charts, diagrams, text, other)?
4. Did you practice with your visuals?

3. Nonverbal delivery skills: how you look and sound
Chapter VII

1. Enhanced body language (posture, gestures, facial expression, and eye contact)?
2. Effective vocal traits (intonation, volume, rate, fillers, and enunciation)?
3. Appropriate use of space and objects around you?
4. Sufficient practice and arrangements?
5. Successful relaxation techniques (either physical, mental, or both)?

CONSULT/JOIN MEETING CHECKLIST

1. Group facilitation: what you say
Chapter V

1. Did you prepare in advance?
   - Objective?
   - Agenda (including purpose and expected participant preparation)?
   - Roles delegated (including perhaps facilitator, timer, and/or scribe)?
2. Did you facilitate participation during the meeting?
   - Effective opening (agenda and ground rules) and closing (decision and action plan)?
   - Encourage participation (effective questions, paraphrases, and listening skills)?
3. Did you end the meeting effectively?
   - Appropriate decision-making technique?
   - Permanent record and action plan?

2. Group facilitation skills: how you listen
Chapter VII

1. Did you use effective attending skills?
   - Posture that shows involvement?
   - Eye contact that signals interest?
   - Distance (how and where you stand or sit)?
2. Did you use effective encouraging skills?
   - Open-ended questions that cannot be answered "yes" or "no"?
   - Door-openers that are nonjudgmental and reassuring?
3. Did you use effective following skills?
   - Paraphrasing both content and perhaps feeling?
   - Recording participant comments?

APPENDIX A

Inclusive Language

Use language that reflects the multicultural reality of business today—language that shows awareness of the global community, that includes rather than excludes, and that is unbiased rather than biased.

Prefer	Avoid
For countries and cultures	
Cultural norms: Most people behave in a certain way most of the time; stated in nonjudgmental, descriptive terms	Stereotypes: All people behave in a certain way all of the time; stated in judgmental, negative terms
Asian	Oriental
United States	America (which could refer to Canada, South America, etc.)
Developing countries	Third World countries
For genders	
Terms that include men and women	Terms that imply that men are the only people in the world
He or she, they or them	He or his (when talking about people in general)
You folks, you people	You guys
Artificial, staff hours	Manmade, man hours
Businessperson, supervisor	Businessman, foreman
Sales representative	Salesman
Dear Sir or Madam:	Dear Sir:
Dear Investment Manager:	Gentlemen:
Dear Customer:	
No salutation, just a subject line, e.g., "Job Opening at XYZ Corporation"	

APPENDIX B

Grammar and Usage

This appendix contains an alphabetical listing of common errors and problems in grammar and usage.

Agreement between pronoun and antecedent

1. Make sure that your pronoun agrees with its antecedent. Use a singular pronoun to refer to antecedents such as *person, woman, man, kind, each, either, neither, another, anyone, somebody, one, everybody,* and *no one.*

    Each of the committee members agrees to complete **his** assignment before the next meeting.

    (To avoid sexist language implicit in the masculine singular pronouns, see Appendix A, on the previous page.)

2. Use the noun nearer the verb to determine the pronoun for subjects joined by *or* or *nor.*

    Neither Julie nor Kara has completed **her** (not *their*) memo.

    Either the manager or her subordinates have made **their** (not *her*) group's proposal.

3. Use a singular pronoun for collective nouns when group is acting in unison.

    The group is preparing **its** (not *their*) statement.

Agreement between subject and verb

1. Make sure your verb agrees with its subject, which may not be the nearest noun.

    The **risks** of a takeover **seem** great.

    The **risk** of a takeover **seems** great.

2. Use the noun nearer the verb to determine the verb for subjects linked by *or* or *nor, either . . . or,* and *neither . . . nor.*

   Either the Art Department or the Editorial Department **has** the copy.

3. Use a singular verb for collective nouns, such as *group, family, committee.*

   The committee **is** meeting after lunch.

4. Use a singular verb for subjects such as *each, either, another, anyone, someone,* something, *one, everybody, no one,* and nothing.

   Each of us **is** . . .

   Another one of the members **has** . . .

   Either of them **decides** . . .

Comma and dash splices

1. Never put two sentences together separated only by a comma or a dash.

   Incorrect comma splice: The company suffers from financial problems, it has great potential in research and development.

   Incorrect dash splice: The company suffers from financial problems—it has great potential in research and development.

2. Watch out for comma and dash splices especially when you use conjunctive adverbs such as *however, therefore,* and *thus.*

   Incorrect comma splice: The company suffers from financial problems, however, it has great potential in research and development.

   Incorrect dash splice: The company suffers from financial problems—however, it has great potential in research and development.

3. Separate comma and dash splices with a period, a semicolon, or a subordinator.

   Separated with period: The company suffers from financial problems. However, it has great potential in research and development.

   Separated with semicolon, implying that the two clauses are of equal importance: The company suffers from financial problems; however, it has great potential in research and development.

   Subordinated first clause, implying that the first clause is less important: Although it suffers from financial problems, the company has great potential in research and development.

See also "Run-on sentences," page 166.

Dangling modifiers

See "Modifiers," below.

Dash splices

See "Comma and dash splices," on the previous page, 162.

Fragments

1. Do not carelessly write a sentence fragment as if it were a complete sentence.

   Incorrect fragment, missing a verb: Especially during the October buying season.

   Incorrect fragment, subordinated subject and verb only: When the October buying season arrives.

2. Occasionally use fragments carefully for emphasis, parallelism, and conversational tone.

   Fragments used correctly for emphasis: Out loud. On your feet. With the remote.

Modifiers

1. To avoid confusing your reader, place your modifiers as close as possible to the words they modify.
2. Avoid unclear modifiers.

   Unclear: The task force seemed sure **on Thursday** the resolution would pass.

   Clear: **On Thursday,** the task force seemed sure . . .

   Clear: The task force seemed sure the resolution would pass **on Thursday.**

3. Avoid "dangling modifiers"—that is, modifiers misplaced at the beginning of your sentence. The opening phrase (before the comma) must refer to the subject of the independent clause.

   Wrong: Young and inexperienced, **the task** seemed easy to Leonard. ("The task" is not "young and inexperienced.")

   Right: Young and inexperienced, **Leonard** thought the task seemed easy.

   Wrong: When calling on a client, **negotiation techniques** are important. ("Negotiation techniques" are not "calling on a client.")

   Right: **Salespeople** calling on a client will find **negotiation techniques** important.

Parallelism

Express ideas of equal importance in grammatical structures of equal importance.

1. Parallel adjectives

   Wrong: She was sensitive and a big help.

   Right: She was sensitive and helpful.

2. Parallel nouns

   Wrong: The new manager is a genius, a leader, and works hard.

   Right: The new manager is a genius, a leader, and a hard worker.

3. Parallel verbs

   Wrong: The workers should arrive on time, correct their own mistakes, and fewer sick days will be used.

   Right: The workers should arrive on time, correct their own mistakes, and use less sick leave.

4. Parallel bullet points

   Wrong: The president announced plans to
   - trim the overseas staff
   - cut the domestic marketing budget
   - better quality control

   Right: The president announced plans to
   - trim the overseas staff
   - cut the domestic marketing budget
   - improve quality control

5. Parallel comparisons

   Wrong: First identifying yourself is more effective than to start right off with your sales pitch.

   Right: First identifying yourself is more effective than starting right off with your sales pitch.

6. Parallel repeated words

   Wrong: He places his laptop, watch, and his money clip on the conveyer belt.

   Right: He places his laptop, his watch, and his money clip on the conveyer belt *or* He places his laptop, watch, and money clip on the conveyer belt.

Pronoun agreement

See "Agreement between pronoun and antecedent," page 161.

Pronoun case

1. *Use the proper case form* to show the function of pronouns in a sentence.

Case Forms

Subjective	I	he/she	you	we	they	who
Objective	me	him/her	you	us	them	whom
Possessive	my (mine)	his/hers	Yours	our (ours)	their (theirs)	whose
Reflexive/ intensive	myself	himself/ herself	yourself	ourselves	themselves	

2. *Use the subjective case* when the pronoun is the subject. Watch out for . . .
   - Compound subjects

     He and **I** finished the job. **We** (not *Us*) managers finished the job.
   - Subject complements

     That may be **she** (not *her*). It was **she who** paid the bill.
3. *Use the objective case* when the pronoun is the sentence object, indirect object, or object of a preposition. Watch out for . . .
   - Sentence objects

     The auditors finally left **him** and **me** (not *he* and *I*).
   - Prepositions

     Just **between you** and **me** (not *you* and *I*) . . .
   - Whom: Use for the object of the sentence, subordinate clause, or preposition.

     Whom did you contact at ABC Company?

     The new chairperson, **whom** we met at the cocktail party, starts work today.

     For **whom** is the message intended?
4. *Use the possessive* to show ownership. Watch out for . . .
   - Gerunds (*-ing* verbs used as nouns)

     We were surprised at **his** (not *him*) resigning.

5. *Use the intensive and reflexive* for emphasis. Watch out for . . .
   - Misuse of *myself:* (Don't use *myself* if you can substitute *I* or *me.*)

     Julia and **I** (not *myself*) designed the market survey.

     He gave the book to Lauren and **me** (not *myself*).

Run-on sentences

1. Never stick two sentences together with a comma, dash, or no punctuation at all.

   Run-on sentence with incorrect comma (comma splice): The company suffers from financial problems, however, it has great potential in research and development.

   Run-on sentence with incorrect dash (dash splice): The company suffers from financial problems—however, it has great potential in research and development.

   Run-on sentence with no punctuation: The company suffers from financial problems however it has great potential in research and development.

2. Separate run-on sentences with a period, a semicolon, or a subordinator.

   Separated with period: The company suffers from financial problems. However, it has great potential in research and development.

   Separated with semicolon, implying that the two clauses are of equal importance: The company suffers from financial problems; however, it has great potential in research and development.

   Subordinated first clause, implying that first clause is less important: Although it suffers from financial problems, the company has great potential in research and development.

Subject–verb agreement

See "Agreement between subject and verb," pages 161–162.

If English is your second language, you may also want to consult *Guide for Internationals: Culture, Communication, and ESL*, cited on page 175.

APPENDIX C

Punctuation

This appendix contains an alphabetical guide to punctuation.

Apostrophe

1. Use an apostrophe to form the possessive of a noun or a pronoun.
   - For nouns (singular or plural) not ending in an *s* or *z* sound, add the apostrophe and *s:*

     Smith's account
     women's rights
     one's own

   - For singular nouns ending in an *s* or *z* sound, add the apostrophe and *s:*

     my boss's office

   - For plural nouns ending in an *s* or *z* sound, add only the apostrophe:

     the Smiths' account
     four dollars' worth

   - For hyphenated compounds, use an apostrophe in the last word only:

     my mother-in-law's idea

   - Differentiate between individual and group possession:

     Garcia and Johnson's account (joint ownership)
     Garcia's and Johnson's accounts (individual ownership)

2. Use an apostrophe to mark the omission of letters in contractions.

they are	they're
fiscal 2010	fiscal '10

3. Use an apostrophe and *s* to form the plural of lowercase letters and of abbreviations followed by periods. When needed to prevent confusion, use the apostrophe and *s* to form the plural of capital letters and abbreviations not followed by periods.

   b's
   M.B.A.'s
   J's or Js
   MBA's or MBAs

4. Do not use an apostrophe with the pronouns *his, its, ours, yours, theirs*, and *whose* or with nonpossessive plural nouns.

   Their department contributed the financial data; ours (not *our's*) added the graphic design.

5. Do not confuse *its* with *it's* or *whose* with *who's*.

   Its filing system is antiquated (its filing system = the filing system of it).

   It's an antiquated filing system (it's = it is).

   She is an accountant **whose** results are reliable (whose results = the results of whom).

   She is an accountant **who's** reliable (who's = who is).

Colon

1. Use a colon as an introducer: to show that what follows will illustrate, explain, or clarify. What follows the colon may be a list, a quotation, a clause, or a word.

   The CEO's decision is final: we will maintain an open-door policy with the press.

   The CEO decided we will do the following: generate a list of potential questions, hold practice interview sessions, and give each person individual feedback after the sessions.

2. Use a colon as a separator between a salutation and the rest of the letter, a title and a subtitle, a chapter and verse of the Bible or Quran, and the hour and the minute.

   Dear Ms. Bourland:

   Guide to Managerial Communication: Effective Business Writing and Speaking

Comma

1. Use a comma to separate independent clauses joined by *and, but, or, nor, for*.

   A long independent clause like this one is perfectly fine, but you need a comma before the coordinator and this second independent clause.

2. Use a comma after introductory transitions and phrases.

   Always use a comma after an introductory transition (such as *however, for example, in the second place*).

   If you find that you have a fairly long introductory phrase at the beginning of your sentence, use a comma before your independent clause (as shown in this sentence).

3. Use a comma to separate items in a parallel series of words, phrases, or subordinate clauses.

   He checked his notes, the projector, and the remote.

4. Use a comma to set off incidental information in the middle of the sentence.

   Incidental information in the middle of the sentence, like this, should be set off with commas.

   Midsentence transitions, moreover, are enclosed in commas.

5. In general, insert a comma whenever you would have a light, natural pause, or whenever necessary to prevent misunderstanding.

Dash

1. Use the dash where you would use a comma when you want a stronger summary or a more emphatic break. Use a dash to emphasize interruptions, informal breaks in thought, or parenthetical remarks—especially if they are strong or contain internal commas.

   Use the dash for a stronger—more emphatic—break.

2. Do not use a dash in place of a period or in place of a semicolon between two independent clauses.

   Do not do this—do not join two complete sentences with a dash.

3. To create a dash—with no space before or after the surrounding words—use the keystroke option.

Exclamation point

Use extremely sparingly to express strong emotions.

Hyphen

1. Use a hyphen between compound adjectives preceding the noun.

   real-time communication
   light-emitting diode

2. Do not use a hyphen if the compound adjective follows the noun.

   communication in real time

3. Do not use a hyphen if the compound adjective makes up an extremely prevalent term.

   venture capital firm

Italics (or underlining)

1. Italics and underlining are used interchangeably for titles, but italics are generally preferred.
2. Use italics for titles of separate publications (books, magazines, and newspapers) and titles of movies, television series, operas, and other long musical compositions.
3. Use italics for unusual foreign words; words, letters, or numbers referred to as such (for example, There are two *m*'s in *accommodate*); and for emphatic typography (see pages 60–61).

Parentheses

1. Use parentheses for unemphatic parenthetical remarks.

   Unlike dashes—which emphasize the importance of what they surround—parentheses minimize the importance (of what they surround).

2. Use parentheses for defining a new term or new abbreviation.

   The Chicago Board Options Exchange (CBOE) provides more liquidity than traditional over-the-counter options markets.

3. Use parentheses to enclose enumerators within a sentence, such as (1) letters and (2) numbers.

4. Punctuate correctly around parentheses.
   - (If an entire sentence is within the parentheses, like this sentence, place the period inside too.)
   - If just part of the sentence is within the parentheses, as in this sentence, place the period or comma outside the parentheses (like this).

Period

1. Use a period to mark the end of declarative sentences.
2. Use a period to mark most abbreviations.
3. Use three spaced periods, called an ellipsis mark, to indicate the omissions of words in a quoted passage. If the omitted material falls at the end of the sentence, the ellipsis should be preceded by a period.

Question mark

Use only after direct questions, not after indirect questions.

Direct question: "What are you doing?"
Indirect question: He asked what I was doing.

Quotation marks

1. Use quotation marks to enclose all direct quotations from speech or writing. Long prose quotations—more than 10 lines—are usually set off by single spacing and indentation and lack quotation marks unless these appear in the original.
2. Use quotation marks to enclose minor titles (short stories, essays, poems, songs, television shows, and articles from periodicals) and subdivisions of books.
3. Use quotation marks to enclose words used in a special sense or quoted from another context.
4. Do not use quotation marks for common nicknames, bits of humor, or trite or well-known expressions.
5. Punctuate correctly around quotation marks.
   - Always place the period and comma within the quotation marks.
   - Always place the colon and semicolon outside the quotation marks.

- Place the dash, the question mark, and the exclamation point within the quotation marks when they apply only to the quoted matter; place them outside when they apply to the whole sentence.

  He called to say, "Your idea stinks!"
  (Punctuation refers to quoted matter only.)
  I can't believe he called back to say, "Actually, I like your idea"!
  (Punctuation refers to the whole sentence.)

6. Use single quotation marks to enclose a quotation or a minor title within a quotation.

   "Use single quotation marks when you have a minor title within a quotation, such as 'Himno Nacional Argentino,' in this quoted sentence."

Semicolon

1. Use a semicolon to join two closely connected independent clauses of equal importance.

   A semicolon indicates a close connection between two independent clauses of equal importance; note that these clauses are not joined by a coordinator *(and, but, or, nor, for).*

2. Use a semicolon to join two independent clauses even if they have a transitional word between them.

   A semicolon indicates a close connection between two independent clauses of equal importance; **however**, don't forget the use of the semicolon to separate independent clauses with a transitional word between them (like *however* in this sentence).

3. Use a semicolon to separate items in a series when your list contains internal commas.

   Use a semicolon to separate items in a series when your list is complex, containing internal commas; when you need stronger punctuation, in order to show where the stronger breaks are; and when you want to avoid confusing your readers, who might get lost with only commas to guide them.

4. Do not use the semicolon to separate items in a list unless the list contains internal commas.

If English is your second language, you may also want to see *Guide for Internationals: Culture, Communication, and ESL*, cited on page 175.

Bibliography

This bibliography is selective, not comprehensive. I included the best references I could find, even if they're not the newest. Some of these articles are "classic"—that is, not recently published but nevertheless crucial—on timeless topics. Others are recent, providing cutting-edge research on more current topics.

Chapter I: Communication Strategy

Communicator Strategy

French, J. and B. Raven, "The Bases of Social Power," in *Studies in Social Power*, D. Cartwright (ed.). Ann Arbor, MI: University of Michigan Press, 1959.

Kotter, J., *Power and Influence*. New York: The Free Press, 1985.

Thompson, M., "The Skills of Inquiry and Advocacy: Why Managers Need Both," *Management Communication Quarterly*, August 1993, 95–106.

Audience Strategy

Cialdini, R., "Harnessing the Science of Persuasion," *Harvard Business Review*, October 2001, 72–79.

Conger, J., "The Necessary Art of Persuasion," *Harvard Business Review*, May 1998, 84–95.

Robbins, S., *Organizational Behavior*, 13th ed. Upper Saddle River, NJ: Prentice Hall, 2009.

Thomas, J., *Guide to Managerial Persuasion and Influence*. Upper Saddle River, NJ: Prentice Hall, 2004.

Williams, G. and R. Miller, "Change the Way You Persuade," *Harvard Business Review*, May 2002, 65–73.

Yates, J., "Persuasion: What the Research Tells Us," Cambridge, MA: MIT Sloan Courseware, 2007.

Message Strategy

Buzan, T. and B. Buzan, *The Mind Map Book*. London, UK: Gardners Books, 2010.

Minto, B., *The Pyramid Principle: Logic in Writing, Thinking and Problem Solving*. London, UK: Minto International, Inc., 2003.

Channel Choice Strategy

DeTienne, K., *Guide to Electronic Communication*. Upper Saddle River, NJ: Prentice Hall, 2002.

Baker, S. and H. Green, "Beyond Blogs," *BusinessWeek*, June 2, 2008, 45–50.

Fahlman, S.E. (who invented smileys in 1982), "Smiley Lore." www.cs.cmu.edu/~sef/sefSmiley.htm

Netlingo, "The List of Chat Acronyms & TM Shorthand." www.netlingo.com/emailsh.cfm

Culture Strategy

Culturgrams. Provo, UT: Kennedy Center Publications, Brigham Young University, published yearly.

Munter, M., "Cross-Cultural Communication for Managers," *Business Horizons*, May–June 1993, 69–79.

Reynolds, S. and D. Valentine, *Guide to Cross-Cultural Communication*, 2nd ed. Upper Saddle River, NJ: Prentice Hall, 2010.

Tannen, D., *Talking From 9 to 5: Women and Men at Work*. New York: Quill, 2001.

Chapters II, III, and IV: Writing

Alred, G. *et al.*, *The Business Writer's Handbook*, 9th ed. New York: St. Martins Press, 2008.

Bringhurst, R., *The Elements of Typographic Style*, 3rd ed. London, UK: Frances Lincoln Ltd, 2005.

Fielden, J., "What Do You Mean You Don't Like My Style?" *Harvard Business Review*, May–June 1982, 128–139.

——— and R. Dulek, "How to Use Bottom-Line Writing in Corporate Communications," *Business Horizons*, July–August 1984, 24–30.

Freeman, L., *Franklin Covey Style Guide for Business and Technical Communication*, 3rd ed. (rev.). Salt Lake City, UT: Franklin Covey Co., 2006.

Munter, M., J. Rymer, and P. Rogers, "Business Email: Guidelines for Users," *Business Communication Quarterly*, March 2003.

Murray, D., *Write to Learn*, 8th ed. Boston, MA: Thomson/Wadsworth, 2005.

Netzley, M. and C. Snow, *Guide to Report Writing*. Upper Saddle River, NJ: Prentice Hall, 2002.

Reynolds, S. and D. Valentine, *Guide for Internationals: Culture, Communication, and ESL*. Upper Saddle River, NJ: Prentice Hall, 2006.

SEC (Securities and Exchange Commission), *A Plain English Handbook*. www.sec.gov/pdf/handbook.pdf

Williams, J., *Style: The Basics of Clarity and Grace*, 4th ed. New York: Longman, 2010.

Chapters V, VI, and VII: Presentations

Atkinson, C. *Beyond Bullet Points*. Redmond, WA: Microsoft Press, 2005.

Baney, J., *Guide to Interpersonal Communication*. Upper Saddle River, NJ: Prentice Hall, 2004.

Bolton, R., *People Skills: How to Assert Yourself, Listen to Others, and Resolve Conflicts*. New York: Simon & Schuster, 1987.

Duarte, N. *slide ology*. Beijing: O'Reilly, 2008.

Howell, J., *Tools for Facilitating Team Meetings*. Seattle, WA: Integrity Publishing, 1995. (Out of print, but worth finding for numerous examples of concept diagrams.)

Jay, A. and R. Jay, *Effective Presentation*, 2nd ed. London, UK: Financial Times Management, 2004.

Knapp, M., *Nonverbal Communication in Human Interaction*, 7th ed. Belmont, CA: Wadsworth/Thomson Learning, 2009.

Kosslyn, S., *Clear and to the Point*. Oxford University Press, 2007.

Linklater, K., *Freeing the Natural Voice*. London, UK: Nick Hern, 2007.

Morgan, N., "How to Become on Authentic Speaker," *Harvard Business Review,* November 2008, 115–119.

Munter, M. and M. Netzley, *Guide to Meetings*. Upper Saddle River, NJ: Prentice Hall, 2002.

——— and D. Paradi, *Guide to PowerPoint* (for PowerPoint Version 2010). Upper Saddle River, NJ: Prentice Hall, 2011.

——— and D. Paradi, *Guide to PowerPoint* (for PowerPoint Version 2007). Upper Saddle River, NJ: Prentice Hall, 2009.

——— and D. Paradi, *Guide to PowerPoint* (for PowerPoint Version 2003). Upper Saddle River, NJ: Prentice Hall, 2007.

——— "How to Conduct a Successful Media Interview," *California Management Review*, Summer 1983, 143–150.

Reynolds, G., *Presentation Zen*. Berkeley: New Riders, 2008.

Russell, L. and M. Munter, *Guide to Presentations,* 3rd ed. Upper Saddle River, NJ: Prentice Hall, 2011.

Schenkler, I. and T. Herrling, *Guide to Media Relations*. Upper Saddle River, NJ: Prentice Hall, 2004.

Tufte, E., *The Cognitive Style of PowerPoint*. Cheshire, CT: Graphics Press, 2003.

———, *The Visual Display of Quantitative Information.* Cheshire, CT: Graphics Press, 2001.

Walker, C., *Learn to Relax: Proven Techniques for Reducing Stress, Tension, and Anxiety*, 3rd ed. New York: Wiley, 2001.

White, J., *Color for Impact: How Color Can Get Your Message Across—or Get in the Way*. Berkeley, CA: Strathmoor Press, 1997.

Williams, R., *The Non-Designer's Design Book: Design & Typographic Principles for the Visual Novice*, 3rd ed. Berkeley, CA: Peachpit Press, 2008.

Zelazny, G., *Say It with Charts: The Executive's Guide to Visual Communication*, 4th ed. New York: McGraw-Hill, 2001.

———, *Say It with Presentations*. New York: McGraw-Hill, 2006.

Index

P

T